ENCYCLOPEDIA OF Extremely WEIRD ANIMALS

Text by Sarah Lovett

John Muir Publications • Santa Fe, New Mexico

John Muir Publications
P.O. Box 613, Santa Fe, New Mexico 87504

Copyright ©1997 by John Muir Publications
All rights reserved.

Printed in the United States of America
First edition. First printing April 1997.

Material in this edition previously published by John Muir Publications
in the *Extremely Weird* series.

Extremely Weird Logo Art: Peter Aschwanden
Illustrations: Mary Sundstrom, Sally Blakemore, Mary Lambert, Beth Evans
Design: Sally Blakemore
Printer: Worzalla, Stevens Point, Wisconsin

ISBN 1-56261-381-2

Contents

MEXICAN FREE-TAILED BAT *(Tadarida brasiliensis)*

Photo, courtesy Merlin D. Tuttle, Bat Conservation Internatic

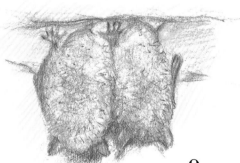

He can climb vertical walls, he can hang from the ceiling, he can see in the dark, he can whizz through the air at speeds of 60 miles per hour. No, it's not Batman, it's a bat. With more than 900 species worldwide, bats are nature's super heroes!

One species of super navigators is the Mexican free-tailed bat. Each night at dusk, giant clouds of these bats emerge from their roosting caves in search of food. Their long, narrow wings are designed for speedy flight and endurance. They stay in the air almost all night long, bolting and darting in pursuit of insects. The largest groups can devour more than 500,000 pounds of insects each night. Take that, Batman!

Mexican free-tails do not hibernate. They stay active all year long. They leave the United States in the fall when the days are short and insects are scarce and winter in Mexico and South America where there's plenty to eat. In their travels, these bats can fly as high as 10,000 feet above the ground (where airplanes fly)!

Yes, Mexican free-tailed bats do have tails, and those tails extend freely beyond the tail membrane, possibly helping them to steer. These North American bats are sociable creatures, and they congregate in the largest colonies of mammals in the world. (Since adults only weigh a half-ounce—with a wingspan of twelve inches—they don't take up much space.) One cave in Texas is home to as many as 20 million bats at one time, each with more natural skills than Batman ever imagined.

Baby free-tails must learn to navigate inside very dark caves while thousands of other bats are jamming the air frequencies with echolocation signals. On its first flight, a young bat might travel 20 feet and avoid several collisions in one second, somersault in midair, and land on a vertical cave wall. Spectacular bat flights can be witnessed most summer evenings and mornings at Carlsbad Caverns National Park in southern New Mexico.

Newborn Mexican free-tailed bats roost separate from their mothers—upside down, side-by-side, sometimes as many as 500 babies per square foot.

Tourists are going batty at the Congress Avenue Bridge in Austin, Texas, which is home to the largest urban bat colony in North America. Between mid-March and early November, about 1.5 million Mexican free-tailed bats emerge at dusk from beneath the bridge and devour tens of thousands of pounds of insects nightly. Crevices underneath the bridge provide perfect homes for female bats to raise their young.

Photo, facing page, courtesy Merlin D. Tuttle, Bat Conservation International

BATS

Fruit bats hanging in a tree (Neg. no. 121314; Courtesy Department Library Services, American Museum of Natural History)

SHORT-TAILED FRUIT BAT *(Carollia perspicillata)*

Nuts about fruit, the short-tailed fruit bat lives in the rain forests of South and Central America where ripe cecropia fruit grow ready-to-eat. Fruit bats also love to munch on piper fruit the same way people eat corn on the cob. That's why they're often called piper-eating bats.

Fruit bats are very important rain forest "farmers." As they fly, these bats scatter the seeds of fruit that will grow into trees and shrubs. In one night, a single short-tailed fruit bat can scatter 60,000 seeds. That's a lot of fruit!

Besides helping to keep rain forests healthy, these bats also replant areas that have been damaged by humans. It is fruit bats who carry and drop the seeds of hearty pioneer plants, the first to grow in areas of the rain forest that have been cleared. In fact, fruit bats are responsible for as much as 90 percent of new growth in cleared areas of tropical forests. Without bats, thousands of other plants and animals would surely disappear.

While fruit-eating bats scatter seeds that grow into new trees and shrubs, nectar-eating bats make sure plants will produce ripe fruit. Some fruit flowers need pollen from other flowers in order to produce fruit. Nectar-eating bats are attracted to the sugary nectar deep inside the flowers. As they feed on nectar, they become dusted with pollen. When they travel to the next flower to feed, they also drop off a little pollen dust, making sure plants will produce fruit.

B A T S

Photo, facing page, courtesy Merlin D. Tuttle, Bat Conservation International

FISHERMAN BAT *(Noctilio leporinus)*

The fisherman bat, a.k.a. the bulldog bat because its cheeky pouches give it a hang-dog look, catches fish on the fly. With ultra-sharp claws, very big feet, and long legs, this Latin American bat spears fish directly from the water. As soon as a fish is hooked, it is scooped into the bat's cheek pouches, where sharp teeth hold the slippery fish until mealtime. Fisherman bats stop at an available perch to eat, or they gobble on the go. A night's catch might be 30 or 40 small fish, crabs, and a variety of winged bugs. Although fisherman bats aren't particularly speedy, their wings are powerful enough to take them on nightly "fishing" trips. Flying in total darkness, they use echolocation (just like insect-eating bats) to detect ripples made by their prey near the surface of rivers, ocean lagoons, and the open sea. Fisherman bat "sonar" is so powerful, they can even detect a human hair poking a fraction of an inch out of water.

Bats are not blind, but at night they often use a system of navigation that works better than sight—it's called echolocation. Just like people, the bat makes a sound with its larynx by causing the air to vibrate. Most bat sounds are too high-pitched for the human ear to hear. The bat sends out pulse after pulse and listens for the echo as the sound bounces back from objects in its path. Scientists believe bats can "sound out" the difference between moths, mosquitoes, and other insects.

BATS

Photo, facing page, courtesy Merlin D. Tuttle, Bat Conservation International

Foxy Hang-Out

GREY-HEADED FLYING FOX *(Pteropus poliocephalus)*

In the tropical forests of eastern Australia, the bats grow on trees. At least it looks that way! When 250,000 lively flying foxes hang out (and upside down) during the day in tree roosts, it's hard to tell the fruit from the bats. These roosting colonies get to be very noisy places, filled with the hubbub of a quarter million bats who squabble, chatter, and move from one spot to another (almost like a game of musical roosts). Indeed, standing underneath a bat-filled tree can be a messy experience because of all the bat droppings raining down.

When the sun sets, these foxy-looking bats follow their noses and eyes to apple, fig, and other fruit trees where they eat, rest, and digest food. Flying foxes use their mouths as "juicers" to squeeze pieces of fruit. They swallow the juice and spit out the seeds and pulp. In this way, seeds are scattered over nearby areas and new trees are planted.

Flying foxes have another "job" besides planting trees: they carry pollen from flower to flower as they feast on nectar. Grey-headed flying foxes are one of the most important pollinators of eucalyptus and other hardwood trees. This bat and its 63 known relatives are busy "gardening" all over the world.

In many parts of the world, flying foxes are responsible for re-seeding and maintaining rain forest diversity. Unfortunately, in spite of their importance to a healthy environment, many countries still allow hunters to kill vast numbers of these bats. Fortunately, some humans are beginning to appreciate how much these bats do for us. The people of southeastern Australia have created a preserve for flying foxes in the green valley of Ku-ring-gai. There, human "bat moms" learn how to care for orphaned and injured bats so they may be returned to the wild.

Photo, facing page courtesy Merlin D. Tuttle, Bat Conservation International

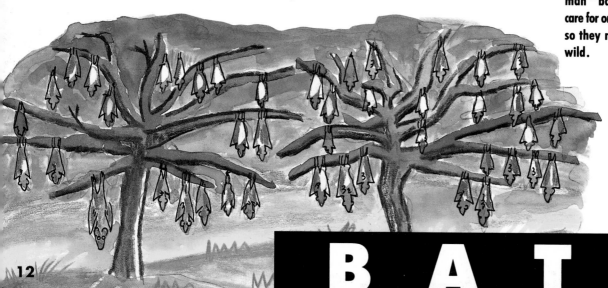

B A T S

LITTLE BROWN BAT *(Myotis lucifugus)*

One of the most common bats in Canada and the northern United States, little brown bats are lightweights—only one-quarter ounce!—and sport thick furry coats ranging in color from reddish to dark brown. Like all bats, they are extremely well groomed. Little browns mate in the fall and then hibernate all winter long in caves or abandoned mines. The sperm of little brown male bats hibernates, too. It stays inactive in the female's body until spring when her egg is fertilized.

Two months later, each female little brown bat gives birth to one baby bat that pulls itself out of its mother's womb. Although bat babies seem tiny to us, they are sometimes one-third the size of their mothers. The human equivalent would be an average-sized human mom giving birth to a 40-pound baby!

Little brown bats must grow up fast—almost within one month—and learn to hunt for insects. When the summer is over, they need enough stored body fat to sleep through the cold winter. Spelunkers (people who explore caves) must be very careful not to disturb colonies of little brown bats and other cave bats. When the bats are hibernating, they go without food, so they must conserve their energy and body fat. If they are disturbed, they fly. If they fly too often during hibernation, they may die from starvation.

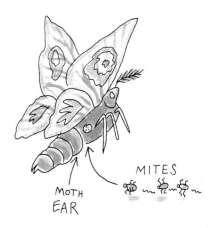

MOTH EAR

MITES

Some moths have learned how to eavesdrop on bat sonar and take evasive action in flight. They hear bat sonar through ears on each side of their body. A tiny mite causes moths to go deaf when it lives as a parasite inside their ears. But the first mite to move in leaves a chemical trail for other mites to follow. The moth lives with one deaf ear and one good ear. In this way, the moth and the mites all avoid becoming dinner for a hungry bat.

Little brown bats form large nursery colonies during the spring and summer, sometimes choosing an abandoned building to set up housekeeping. People often accuse little brown bats of being a nuisance, but these bats hardly ever pose health problems to humans.

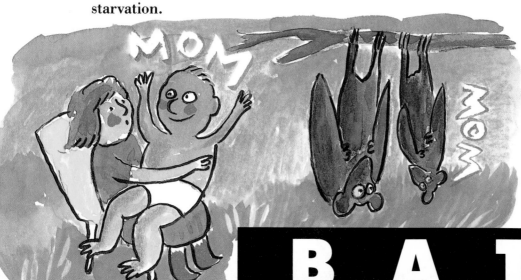

MOM

B A T S

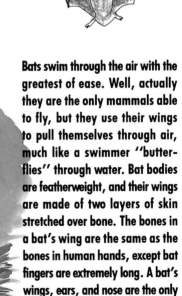

To Croak or Not to Croak?

FROG-EATING BAT *(Trachops cirrhosus)*

Flying on night missions, amazing frog-eating bats locate frogs by their call—they can also tell who's bite-sized and who's poisonous. These bats, living in the tropical forests from Mexico to southern Brazil, cause problems for male frogs—how to call for a mate but not a hungry bat.

Most bat hearing is adapted to the high-frequency signals used for echolocation. Frog-eating bats have another type of hearing—low-frequency—that picks up the loudest frog calls. These particular bats have developed this ability through evolution. As the bats slowly change, so do the frogs.

Frog-eating bats have encouraged frogs to learn new survival tactics. Some male frogs have developed mating calls that make it harder for bats (and female frogs) to locate them. Other frogs keep quiet on dark nights since they can't use their eyes to see, and frogs have no "sonar" to warn them of hungry bats.

Bats swim through the air with the greatest of ease. Well, actually they are the only mammals able to fly, but they use their wings to pull themselves through air, much like a swimmer "butterflies" through water. Bat bodies are featherweight, and their wings are made of two layers of skin stretched over bone. The bones in a bat's wing are the same as the bones in human hands, except bat fingers are extremely long. A bat's wings, ears, and nose are the only body parts not covered with fur.

B A T S

Photo, facing page, courtesy Merlin D. Tuttle, Bat Conservation International

LITTLE YELLOW-EARED BAT *(Vampyressa pusilla)*

With a head and body that is about as long as a human thumb and ears that are yellowish, the little yellow-eared bat lives up to its name. This bat's nose has a small horn that sticks straight up, giving it the look of a tiny, flying rhinoceros. Why do many bats have lumps, bumps, giant ears, and weird facial growths? Scientists believe these odd wrinkles help bats echolocate by directing outgoing and incoming sound waves. Most high-frequency sounds that bats use in echolocation can't be heard by the human ear, but we can hear some sociable sounds that bats use to communicate while roosting.

The little yellow-eared bat prefers humid areas of evergreen forests in southern Mexico, Peru, and parts of Brazil. It roosts in trees and shrubs and dines mostly on fresh fruit.

Bat detectors let you "see" bats with your ears. These instruments are designed to change high-pitched bat signals to sounds that humans can hear. With practice, listeners learn to decipher a "feeding buzz" from a "landing buzz" and the putt-like sound of big brown bats from the chirping call of hoary bats. All you need is patience and a city park to learn more about your neighborhood bats.

Photo, facing page, courtesy Merlin D. Tuttle, Bat Conservation International

BATS

Tutti Fruitti

JAMAICAN FRUIT-EATING BAT *(Artibeus jamaicensis)*

Latin American fruit-eating bats are nutty about mangoes, bananas, figs, avocados, and espave nuts. After dark, these bats carry small fruit to special places where they eat, but toward morning, they return to their regular roosts with a cargo of fresh fruit. It doesn't take long for fruit to pass through a hungry bat—only about 15 to 20 minutes. Scientists believe the fruit is digested with enzymes or chemicals, because there isn't enough time for bacteria to go into action. Fruit-eating bat droppings often smell like fruit, and these bats scatter piles of seeds, nuts, and fruit rinds beneath their roosting sites. In this way, they plant new fruit trees.

Female fruit-eaters give birth twice a year, probably because they have a breeding season that is longer than usual. Although a few species of bats commonly have twins and this is only once a year, most bats have only one baby per year. That means it takes a long time for bat populations to increase or recover from destruction.

Although bats live in most areas of the world, they are especially plentiful in the tropical forests. These forests are biological treasure chests containing more than 90% of *all* land-dwelling plant and animal species. They are also vital to the balance of our world climates. Making life choices that promote rain forest conservation is one way we can all ensure a healthy future for Planet Earth.

BATS

Photo, facing page, courtesy Merlin D. Tuttle, Bat Conservation International

WAHLBERG'S EPAULETED BAT *(Epomophorus wahlbergi)*

When she was eleven years old, Camellia Ibrahim began a log to keep track of a small colony of Wahlberg's epauleted bats that were sharing her house in Kenya, Africa. When Camellia wrote to Bat Conservation International for more information, she discovered that very little is known about these bats. Her journal shares firsthand observations with those of us who aren't lucky enough to have bats for roommates.

Camellia's Log I got up at 20 minutes to six so I could see the bats come in this morning. It was still quite dark, but our porch lamp showed them quite well. The scene under our eaves looked like a busy airport!

The bats all used the same flight path. Some hovered to inspect roosting quarters and others had squeaky quarrels over territory.

March 8, 1987 There are 10 bats today. A mother and baby have a "room" all to themselves. The mother, Helen, holds the baby, which I have named Coffee, in her wings so you can only see the baby's head. She licks it often.

April 20 We have wondered how bats, hanging upside down

Reprinted with permission from BATS, BCI Vol. 6 (1), Spring 1988.

(or rightside down to them!), can make their toilet without dirtying themselves. Today we watched Tander do it. He used the extended thumb on his wings to hang on and let go with his feet. Then he turned the rest of his body down. When he finished, he brought his feet up again and let go with his wings.

May 7 28 adults and 1 baby. Fawn and Toto are still together, but Coffee has left his mother. He now roosts by himself, but still near his mother.

Bat Conservation International (BCI) can give you more information on bats. This nonprofit organization funds worldwide bat education and conservation projects. They also publish *BATS*, a newsletter for members of all ages. For a donation of any size, you can receive easy-to-follow bat house plans. Write to BCI at P.O. Box 162603, Austin, TX 78716.

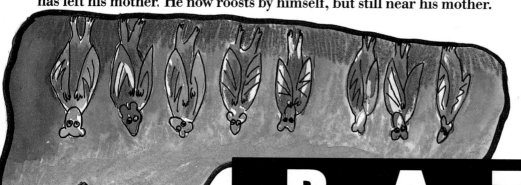

BATS

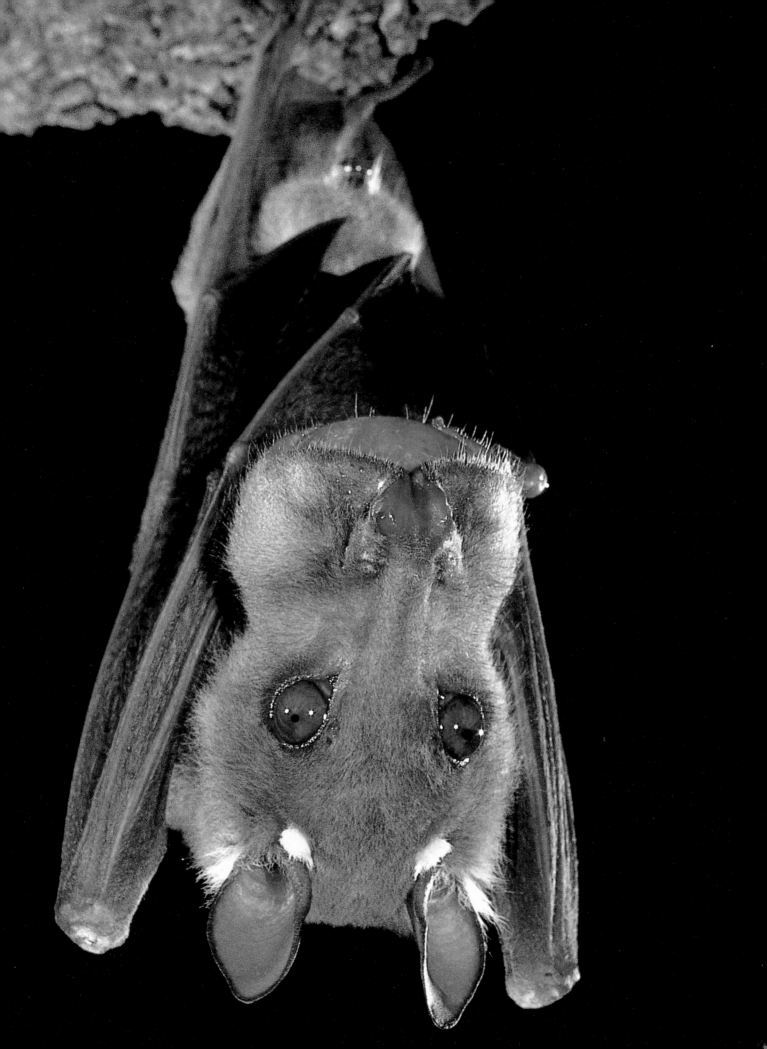

GOTHIC BAT *(Lonchorhina aurita)*

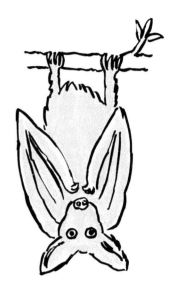

You might say it looks like a tiny cathedral, or maybe a stone gargoyle come to life. Either way, the reddish-brown Gothic bat has a very impressive sword-nose that is almost as long as its ears. From southern Mexico to Peru, Brazil, and Trinidad, this bat hangs out in caves and tunnels where the weather is humid and the trees are thick. And even with its fierce face, the Gothic bat is an easygoing critter.

Gothic bats often share their roosts with short-tailed fruit bats. As long as there is room in a tunnel for one group in front and the other in back, everyone seems happy. Occasionally, Gothic bats are loners who hang from trees and walls by themselves.

Bats spend most of their daytime lives roosting—that includes grooming, mating, raising babies, and socializing. Even at night, bats rest and digest at their roosting sites. Hibernating bats may roost for three months at a time. Besides caves, tunnels, and other dark places, bats sometimes choose to hang out in hollow trees, bushes, attics, and empty buildings. In fact, almost any nook or cranny will do for a tired bat.

A bat hang-out is really a bat hang-upside-down. Most bats roost by hanging from their toes, which lock into place when the bat's entire weight is suspended from them. Once "locked in," bats may fall asleep without danger of falling. Cave-dwelling bats also use their thumb-claws to anchor themselves to the ceiling. A few bats even have tiny suction cups on their wrists and feet to grip leaves and stems of plants. Bats' knees are on "backward," which helps them move around their roost.

:ing page, courtesy Merlin D. Tuttle, Bat Conservation International

FALSE VAMPIRE BAT *(Vampyrum spectrum)*

People used to believe that the false vampire bat, from the tropical forests of Latin America, drank the blood of animals just like true vampire bats. Actually, this bat is one of a few bat species that are omnivorous (they eat meat, too). The false vampire bat lives on the flesh of small rodents, birds, and other bats as well as insects and fruit. When eating mice, false vampire bats chew the head first, the body second, and then throw out the tail.

This is a very big bat, as bats grow. It has a body length of about 5 inches and a wingspan of almost 3 feet.

Hollow tree trunks are the favorite roosting sites for small groups of false vampire bats, although they sometimes choose churches and other available buildings.

In scientific studies, captive false vampire bats are easy to tame and become very gentle. In fact, bats in general are surprisingly docile, shy, and easy to train. Of course, like all wild creatures, bats should be handled with care—and only by experts. Never try to capture a downed bat by yourself—it may be sick or injured.

Dracula, vampire, ghost, demon! Because bats hunt at night in complete darkness, superstitious people have long feared their "supernatural powers." As we learn more about the world, bats have revealed their gentle and beneficial nature, and "supernatural" powers have turned out to be extremely natural!

B A T S

EGYPTIAN FRUIT BAT *(Rousettus aegyptiacus)*

Shrill screams, hacking coughs, and the squabbling of bumper-to-bumper bats—this is the noise of Egyptian fruit bats roosting in ancient tombs and temples, trees, date palms, or caves. This might sound almost scary, but it's business as usual for fruit bats in Turkey, Pakistan, Egypt, and most of Africa south of the Sahara Desert. From their day roosts, Egyptian fruit bats probably travel small distances at night to find plenty of fruit juice and flower nectar, their favorite feast.

Because fruit bats poke their noses into flowers, they pick up and deliver pollen from one tree to another. While feeding, they are also making sure the plant produces fruit and seeds so there will be new plants in the following years.

Egyptian fruit bats mate from June through September, and females give birth four months later. Newborn babies are carried by their mothers until they're old enough to be left behind in the roost. Within three or four months, young Egyptian fruit bats can navigate on their own.

Egyptian fruit bats are important pollinators of the baobab flower. So many animals depend on the baobob tree for food and shelter that it is also called "the tree of life." If not for the fruit bat, these trees might disappear, triggering a chain of related extinctions.

While early American and European artists often painted bats as devils and demons, Chinese art is filled with lucky, healthy, blissful bats. Ancient Chinese scholars thought bats lived to old age because "they swallowed their breath" in deep dark caves. Artists in China still use five bats to represent five blessings: health, long life, prosperity, love of virtue, and a peaceful death.

BATS

CHAPIN'S FREE-TAILED BAT *(Tadarida chapini)*

Chapin's free-tails (from Africa) are especially known for their "hairdos." Male Chapin's bats sport a flashy two-colored crest between their ears, but females are plainer and do without punk locks. This difference between the sexes is not unusual in bats and other animals. Like male bats of many species, male Chapin's bats have specialized scent glands that are used as mating signals to attract females. These scent glands are located underneath the handsome crest, and the hairs help spread the sexy odor. Of course, it won't smell like cologne to our human noses, but the musk scent is bat perfume. Many species of flying foxes also use this technique, including the straw-colored flying fox, which has a rusty orange-colored patch of fur on its throat just above a scent gland.

Winter puts the skinny on bats. During months of hibernating, body fat keeps bats warm and nourished. As fat gets used up, a bat's body will shrink until it loses almost one-third its body weight!

Bat mothers give birth hanging upside down! Babies are tiny, naked, wrinkled, and born with a full set of teeth. Their itsy bitsy teeth are hook-shaped to stick tight to their mother's nipples.

Bats are worldly creatures. They live on every continent except Antarctica.

B A T S

30

Mini-bat

KITTI'S HOG-NOSED BAT *(Craseonycteris thonglongyai)*

This teensy bat, named for its Miss Piggy nose, is the smallest bat in Thailand as well as one of the smallest mammals in the entire world!

Because the hog-nosed bat is only the size of a large bumblebee, it's also called the bumblebee bat.

Hog-nosed bats, insect-eating cave-dwellers, are now endangered, probably because their roosting and feeding areas are being damaged by humans. In the area where the hog-nosed bat lives, many trees and plants have been cut down.

These tiny bats, which fit into the palm of your hand, need the help of conservationists to survive environmental hazards caused by humans. Although hog-nosed bats are found only in Thailand, conservationists from all over the world are working to save this very special bat.

Who's endangered? Every year, the International Union for the Conservation of Nature (IUCN) updates its list of endangered plant and animal species worldwide. Scientists believe that many species not on the endangered list should be. Unfortunately, some bat species are so shy they are rarely seen by humans and very little is known about them. No one even knows if they're endangered!

Assorted sizes. The tiniest bat is Kitti's hog-nosed with a wingspan of 5½ inches. The biggest bat is a flying fox with a wing spread of 5½ feet!

Bumblebee bat bodies are about the size of a jelly bean or a hazelnut, and they weigh less than a dime!

ATLANTIC PUFFIN (*Fratercula arctica*)

What stands ten inches tall, has a large red bill, red feet and legs, and holes in its head? What else but an Atlantic puffin!

Atlantic puffins are shorebirds and relatives of auks, dovekies, and murres. True to their name, puffins live along the North Atlantic coast and feed on fish. They mate during the spring. Afterward, they shed the surface of their brightly colored bill.

Like other birds, a puffin's skull is full of holes. In fact, many of the bones of a bird's skeleton are hollow. Holey, hollow bones are lighter, and they make it easier for birds to balance. Of course, bird bones must be strong as well as light. Bones that are tube-shaped (like straws) have thin, crosswise supports inside, resembling honeycomb. Other bones contain air sacs that are connected to the lungs. These "balloons" make birds even lighter and increase oxygen flow. Another plus: birds like the Atlantic puffin are equipped with bills instead of teeth. Bird bills are horny (not bony), and they weigh grams instead of kilograms. If you're always on the ground, like humans, elephants, and horses, you can afford a heavy skeleton, but fliers must be lightweights, or featherweights!

Because birds don't have teeth, their food is broken down during digestion. Plant-eating birds depend on a small muscular organ called the gizzard to grind up food. The gizzard is often aided by small stones that the bird swallows.

A puffin "flies" underwater, turns its head from side to side, and picks fish from a school until its beak is filled to capacity!

Photo, facing page, courtesy Lincoln Nutting/Photo Researchers, Inc.

Eagle Eye

HARPY EAGLE (*Harpia harpyja*)

Hawks, vultures, falcons, and ospreys are all diurnal birds of prey—raptors that are active during the day. So are eagles. There are more than 200 species of these meat-eaters occupying most of the world except for Antarctica and Oceania.

Raptors come in a variety of sizes—from the pygmy falcon (about the size of a smallish dove) to the huge Andean condor, which has a 10-foot wingspan. Most raptors have a bill that is a sharp hook and feet that are powerful and equipped with razor-edged talons. Females are often larger than their mates, and usually both sexes share in the duties of nest-building, egg incubation, feeding, and protection of the young.

The harpy eagle from South America may qualify as one of the world's strongest birds of prey. The harpy lives on the edges of rain forests and hunts capuchin, squirrel, and woolly monkeys as well as sloths and tree porcupines, which it tears from the branches using its talons. Harpy eagles have even been known to kill small dogs and baby pigs.

They are solitary hunters, and males and females pair up only during courtship. Harpies line their treetop nests with leaves, ferns, moss, and the bones of their prey. Males are allowed in nest territory only long enough to drop off food for the female and her young.

Native people have long valued the harpy eagle's feathers. The shiny white, gray, and black plumes are exchanged for food and other items.

Hawks and eagles are famed for their keen eyesight. Their retinas are chock-full of visual cells—eight times as many as people have. High-flying at 10,000 feet above ground, we humans could just make out a pronghorn antelope if we looked very closely. At the same distance, most birds of prey would see it clearly, at a glance.

Eagles, hawks, and other birds of prey swoop down on their prey and use their long talons to tear or strike.

Peregrine falcons, the world's speediest birds, have been clocked pursuing prey in dives of 175 miles per hour! They slash their victims with razor-sharp claws and force them to the ground.

Photo, facing page, courtesy Tom McHugh/Photo Researchers, Inc.

The Better to Hear Whooooo?

Owls are so flexible, they can look at the world with an upside-down head!

ORIENTAL BAY OWL (*Phodilus badius*)

Owls are carnivores, which means they eat other animals such as spiders, insects, crustaceans, fish, frogs, rodents, and birds. Since most owls are nocturnal (night) hunters, nature has provided some fancy equipment for locating prey after dark. Owl eyes and sockets are big, and the owl's eyesight is keen. But they depend most on excellent hearing for their hunting edge. The disk-like shape of the owl's face—enhanced by hard, wiry feathers—helps direct sound. The disk serves the same function as the external earflaps of most mammals. Other birds only have ear holes.

Owls also depend on silence and surprise to ensure a successful hunt. Their flight feathers are set in a loose weave and fringed with special barbs or "sound dampers" for silent attacks on unsuspecting prey. These powerful hunters have strong legs and sharp curved talons (claws) that make it possible to grasp their prey.

Most small and medium-sized owls nest in trees. They sometimes choose holes excavated by woodpeckers or other animals. Larger owls may build nests of grass, feathers, and twigs or borrow stick nests abandoned by hawks, crows, and other birds. In most species, the male is responsible for feeding his mate and offspring from the time incubation begins until the young fledge. Often, the female is much larger than the male.

Oriental bay owls live in parts of northern India, Sri Lanka, and Southeast Asia. Adults are almost 12 inches (29 cm) tall and feed mostly on insects. They raise three to five young in their nests built in tree hollows.

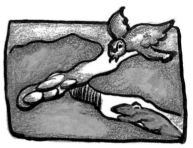

Some burrowing owls use the spare tunnels of the predatory badger for raising their young. Manure, packed into the burrow by the bird, probably keeps the badger from smelling the nest.

Head backward! An owl's eyes are positioned on the front of its face, like a human's eyes. For this reason, owls can't see to the side as easily as other birds. Not without turning their heads, that is. Owls can move their heads in half circles in either direction so they look as if they're on backward!

Photo, facing page, courtesy Tom McHugh/Photo Researchers, Inc.

BIRDS

SINGLE-WATTLED CASSOWARY (*Casuarius unappendiculatis*)

Birds fly. At least most of them do. But there are some birds who spend all their time on the ground. Flightless birds can be divided into two groups: those whose ancestors flew at one time (penguins, for example) and those whose ancestors probably never flew (such as the cassowary).

Since the ancestors of some birds may have given up flight millions of years ago, how does anybody know for sure who flew and who didn't? Ornithologists (people who study birds) know that most birds have a keel-shaped sternum (breastbone) that juts out like the bottom of a boat. This shape means there is lots of room for large flight muscles to attach to the bone. Although penguins are flightless, their sternum *is* keeled, and their wing stroke under water is mechanically identical to an aerial wing stroke. Flightless cassowaries, in contrast, have flat sternums. In fact, cassowaries are also known as "ratites," which means raftlike, or flat.

Huge single-wattled cassowaries grow to a height of 5 feet, and they can run at 30 miles per hour, leap, and swim, but they can't get off the ground. Not with their wings, that is. Cassowaries use their smallish wings to ward off sticks and branches when they sprint through the forests of New Guinea and Australia, where they live. They eat fruits, insects, and plants. Because they're grounded, cassowaries defend themselves with long, slashing, razorlike nails on their inner toes.

The female cassowary deposits four or five giant, green eggs on a nest of leaves at the foot of a tree. From then on, her mate must incubate, brood, feed, and care for the young.

What's a wattle? That weird, fleshy, wrinkly, often brightly colored flap of skin that adorns the faces of certain birds such as the cassowary.

The ostrich (another ratite) is the world's biggest living bird! Eight feet tall from head to both toes, the adult ostrich can race along at 40 (even 45!) miles per hour.

Moas are extinct birds that looked like pin-headed ostriches. These giants could reach a height of 12 feet and weighed more than 500 pounds. Moas used to live in New Zealand.

Pasta Penguin

MACARONI PENGUIN (*Eudyptes chrysolophus*)

Clumsy on land, penguins are masters of watery motion—capable of swan dives into frigid seas and of powerful strokes with flipperlike wings. There are seventeen species of penguins, all flightless, all more or less medium- to large-sized. They are found in Antarctic seas all the way to the equator. Their legs, tail, and neck are short, and their feet are flat and webbed. They stand erect on land and propel like bullets in water.

A black tuxedo and spiked headgear give the macaroni penguin a punk appearance and its unusual name. This bird lives by and in the southern Atlantic and Indian oceans.

In the swim, penguins execute a kind of underwater flight with their wings doing all the work. Their bodies are layered with fat and covered with three layers of scalelike feathers that act as natural wetsuits. They are the most aquatic of all birds!

Although penguins live around the edges of Antarctica, some species, like the Adélie penguin, breed inland and must march (or toboggan on their bellies) miles and miles to and from the sea to find food.

Warm feats! Male emperor penguins incubate the egg and the young while the female goes to sea—sometimes for as long as 2 months. The father tucks the egg between his feet and his belly. Baby emperor penguins stand on their parents' large webbed feet and snuggle into the belly warmers. Babies hatch on their dad's toes.

Birds have 6 basic types of feathers—contour, filoplume, semiplume, powder down, down, and bristle. Soft down feathers are found on young birds and some adult birds. Filoplumes are found around the bills of some perching birds. Contour feathers give the bird its shape. Bristles are hairlike feathers found around a bird's mouth or eyes.

BROWN PELICAN (*Pelecanus occidentalis*)

The pelican is known for its enormous beak that holds more than its belly can. Actually, the lower beak has an expandable skin pouch, which is filled and filled and filled with fish. White pelicans dine on fresh-water fish from marshes, lagoons, and lakes. Brown pelicans, in contrast, feed only in salt water. They have developed a special skill for fishing.

The brown pelican is a high-diver extraordinaire. From a height of 20 meters (more than 60 feet) or less, it plunges straight downward or in a spiral, with its head close to its body and wings partly folded, to strike the water head first and disappear. Then, after pouch-netting fish, it pops up again like a bobbing cork.

Although they are aerial acrobats, swooping, gliding, and floating on the air currents, pelicans have trouble when it comes to takeoffs. They're not really heavy, but they are large. They solve the problem of size by running full-speed-ahead, webbed paddle feet slapping the water's surface.

Brown pelicans spend their lives on both coasts of North America and the west coast of South America. In crowded, busy colonies they breed and nest on islands where there are few predators. Although mature pelicans can be noisy—they hiss, blow, groan, and sometimes clatter their beaks together—the young *really* create a din. Barking, squeaking, bleating, grunting, and groaning are all part of a young pelican's vocabulary.

White pelicans team up to catch fish! Forming a line, pelicans paddle forward, driving fish to shallow waters where they are easily pouched up.

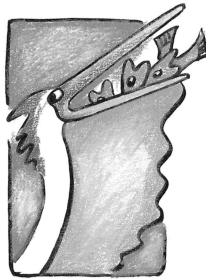

An adult pelican can devour more than 10 pounds of fish per day!

A pelican parent's bill may be five times as long as its newly hatched youngster. And an adult pelican's wing can span 9 feet!

Anhingas, or "snake-birds," have sharp beaks made for spearing fish. When the anhinga tosses its meal overhead, it can catch it with open beak, just like you catch peanuts!

Photo, facing page, courtesy Carl Purcell/Photo Researchers, Inc.

B I R D S

Sky Surfers

MAGNIFICENT FRIGATEBIRD (*Fregata magnificens*)

Frigatebirds are far-out fliers, soaring, gliding, wheeling, and riding the air currents like surfers of the sky. Also known as man-o'-war birds, frigates use their aerial skills to snatch meals from other birds. A pelican, booby, tern, cormorant, or gull harassed by a high-flying frigatebird will finally drop its food. The frigatebird then dives swiftly to catch its borrowed meal in midair.

Frigatebirds are seabirds that can be found in tropical and subtropical oceans where flying fish (one of their favorite meals) are common. Frigatebirds do cruise out to sea, but generally they stay close to their island breeding grounds. They are gregarious birds, and they breed year-round in large colonies.

Male frigatebirds develop a bright red, balloonlike throat sac when courting females. They perch proudly in nesting areas of the colony, throat sac inflated (for hours at a time!), shiny black wings spread, to attract flying females. As if that's not enough to impress a potential mate, the males shake and rattle their long, hooked beaks.

Icarus flew too close to the sun and his wings melted—according to ancient legend, that is! It's a great story, but the real story is that humans just don't have the muscle power for flapping flight!

Flying fossil! *Pteranodon*, a prehistoric pterodactyl reptile, was the biggest flying animal ever! Its wings spanned 25 feet (7.5 m), and they were covered with webbed skin instead of feathers. *Pteranodon* was a gliding flier, not a flapping flier.

How big is an egg? Most of us are familiar with chicken eggs, but what about an ostrich egg? One egg can be as big as a cantaloupe and weigh more than 4,000 hummingbird eggs.

Photo, facing page, courtesy George Holton/Photo Researchers, Inc.

BIRDS

SOUTHERN BALD IBIS (*Geronticus calvus*)

Ibises, like storks, flamingos, herons, and jabirus, are long-legged waders. These birds live in colonies in most marshy tropical areas of the world. Their long, narrow beaks curve downward and are handy for picking insects, crabs, mollusks, and worms from mud and dirt. Sometimes, ibises catch larger prey such as frogs and small rodents. These quick critters have even been known to snap hummingbirds from midair.

In flight, ibises alternate wing strokes with gliding movements, and all birds in a flock seem to make their moves together.

Generally, the ibis has sturdy legs of medium length (about 12 inches), and its neck and face are bare of feathers. The southern bald ibis lives in parts of South Africa. Its relative, the northern bald ibis, lives in North Africa and Europe. Other species include the sacred ibis, scarlet ibis, hermit ibis, and wattled ibis.

The ostrich has two large toes on each foot, and these are handy for dashing across soft African sand. Scientists believe that eventually, the ostrich might have only one toe, just like a horse! That's a foot of evolution for you!

Photo, facing page, courtesy M. P. Kahl/Photo Researchers, Inc.

Flying dino! A bird's keeled breastbone is made to attach flight muscles. Its shoulder joints are made for flapping. Otherwise, some dinosaur skeletons and the skeletons of the first flying birds aren't all that different. Both had tails, and both had air sacs to lighten their bodies.

BIRDS

Hummmm-dinger!

BROAD-BILLED HUMMINGBIRD (*Cynanthus latirostris*)

Who takes the cake as the world's smallest birds? Hummingbirds, ah hummmmmm! They are also some of the most colorful, boasting a rainbow of shiny iridescent feathers. Hummingbirds (a.k.a. hummers) are also nifty navigators capable of aerial feats and famed for their power strokes. While most birds use a power stroke (usually the down-stroke) alternating with a recovery stroke (usually the upstroke), hummingbirds hover by using power strokes all the time, both down and up. In fact, hummingbirds can flap their wings more than 80 times per second. That takes lots of energy!

In flight (and they almost always are), hummingbirds move like minute hovercraft. They hover and fly backward, and their wings move so quickly they're just a blur of motion. Because they spend so little time on solid ground, hummingbird feet are teensy and weak.

Hummers often have very lonnngggg bills—long enough to reach deep into flowers. Their tongues, shaped like thin straws, are handy for sucking nectar from flowers. Hummingbirds also devour extremely tiny insects.

There are more than 300 species of hummingbirds. Broad-billed hummingbirds spend summers in the southwestern United States and winters in Mexico. They prefer desert canyons and foothills where agaves and mesquite grow. Dark green with a blue throat and a bright red, black-tipped bill, adults reach a length of just 4 inches (10 cm).

Costa's hummingbird builds a tiny nest of plants and lichen and wraps it with a spider's web!

Hummingbirds are the only birds able to fly backward and sideways!

It's no surprise the world's tiniest bird lays the world's teensiest eggs. Hummingbirds always lay two eggs, each the size of a Tic Tac candy.

Photo, facing page, courtesy G. C. Kelley/Photo Researchers, Inc.

BIRDS

A Shoe Fit

SHOEBILL STORK (*Balaeniceps rex*)

One of the weirdest storks of all is the shoebill, and if you use your imagination, this stork's thick, high bill does look a bit like unusual footwear. It has also been described as a "whale-headed" stork, and, in fact, that's what its scientific name means. It may even resemble some birds you've seen in cartoons.

Shoebills are found only in the marshlands of tropical Africa where they spend their days near rivers or grassy flood areas. Their bootlike bills—8 inches long and almost as wide—are perfect for probing in muddy water. They eat river fish, frogs, and snails, and they prefer to hunt for food at night. These shy birds are ground nesters, and they usually lay two eggs in flat grassy areas. Like all storks, shoebills are able fliers.

The shoebill stork has a tiny comb built into its central toenail which it uses to "comb" its feathers. Birds do not have oil glands in their skin like humans do. Instead, they have a preen gland located at the base of their tails. They also have powder down (feathers that have turned to powder), which they use with the oil to groom and waterproof their feathers.

Storks are mute because they have no voicebox. Storks clatter their bills to get their point across.

Photo, facing page, courtesy Jeffry Ferraro/Photo Researchers, Inc.

GROUND HORNBILL (*Bucorvus leadbeateri*)

Boasting a swollen 9-inch-long bill, a frill of long eye-lashes, and a red or blue inflatable throat sac, the ground hornbill is as large and as weird-looking as a turkey. This long-legged bird is the most terrestrial (ground-dwelling) of all the hornbill species. It lives in the savannas of Africa. There, this omnivorous bird hunts for insects, reptiles, mice, and other bird's eggs.

Ground hornbills often nest in hollow trees or cracks and crevices in cliffs, and the female may come and go as she pleases during incubation and rearing of young. That's not the case in most species.

When females of the black dwarf hornbills, rhinoceros hornbills, and others settle down, they are real stay-at-homes. First, a mating hornbill pair chooses a nest site in a tall tree with a hollow cavity. The female lays large white eggs, which she begins to incubate. Eventually, her mate starts to bring home bits of mud and earth, and the female mixes these with bird-droppings and regurgitated food to seal herself inside the nest hole. When the seal is complete, there is only enough room for the tip of her bill to fit through the small opening. This barrier appears to keep predators away from the female and her young, but it leaves the male with a very big job. He must supply food for the female during the 30 to 40 days of incubation. After the young hatch, he may have to feed them all for weeks, even months, until the female feels it's time to escape!

The African jacana is also known as the lily-trotter because it tiptoes over floating lily pads. By spreading its toes, it also spreads out its body weight.

Ornithologists study fossils to understand how different species of birds have evolved or changed over the eons. Archaeopteryx, one of the earliest feathered animals, left a semireptilian print in fossils. It had feathers and could glide but probably spent most of its time on the ground. Was it a bird? Not really. Was it a dinosaur? Probably not. In fact, some scientists believe it may belong to its very own group.

B I R D S

Hop-a-long and Headfirst

MADAGASCAR MALACHITE KINGFISHER (*Alcedo cristata vintsioides*)

There are more than 80 known species of kingfishers, and they can be as little as 5 inches or as big as 1½ feet. Kingfishers are divided into two large groups—wood kingfishers and true kingfishers. While wood kingfishers are usually found in forests far from water, true kingfishers spend their active days near streams, rivers, and lakes.

Breeding pairs guard their territory and keep other kingfishers away. They hunt by diving headfirst into water from their hunting perches or from midair like hovercraft. They eat live prey such as fish and water insects.

True kingfishers nest in holes in sandy riverbanks and streambanks and lake slopes. They use their three fused front toes as scoopers to push out soil already loosened by their long, narrow beak. Sometimes, their nests are as deep as one meter (about 3 feet).

When breeding pairs court in the spring, the male brings a gift. He offers his mate a fish, head first (just as the young will be fed). The female lays between six and eight eggs, and when the young hatch, they need tiny fish on their first day of life. Each young kingfisher eats about six fish per day, gulped whole.

Give me a brake! Landing birds lower and fan their tail feathers to use them as air brakes as they approach a perch.

Geese and some other water birds use their webbed feet to run across water for takeoffs and landings.

Photo, facing page, courtesy Photo Researchers, Inc.

B I R D S

GREATER PRAIRIE CHICKEN (*Tympanuchus cupido*)

Known for their courting rituals, greater prairie chickens are said to have inspired many dances of Great Plains Native Americans. Each spring, the male birds return to traditional dancing sites or "booming grounds" to court females. With neck feathers erect and neck sacs inflated like great orange balloons, they strut, shuffle, and make booming noises.

The sharptail grouse, a relative of the prairie chicken, participates in similar courtship dances. Males shuffle and stamp their feet quickly, heads up and tails down. And they all start and stop at once, on a dime.

Many birds have courting rituals, and some even molt (shed) their regular feathers and grow new, showier, spiffier plumes just for the occasion. A courting male works to impress a female of the species so she will choose him as her mate.

Unfortunately, much of the greater prairie chicken's habitat has been developed for farmland. These birds are an endangered species threatened with extinction.

People use birds as symbols. Doves stand for peace, bluebirds mean happiness, eagles are brave, and owls are wise. Has anyone ever called you a bird brain?

A grouse will fly-dive head first into a snowbank to insulate itself from the cold. Think of it as a bird igloo.

Birds are incredible commuters. They can cross continents and seas during migration. Some migrating geese are known to travel 2,000 miles at 35 miles per hour in three days. Ducks are even faster: they cover 1,000 miles per day at 40 miles per hour.

Photo, facing page, courtesy R. Van Nostrand/Photo Researchers, Inc.

BIRDS

KORI BUSTARD (*Ardeotis kori*)

Bustards have been around for years—at least 50 million years, in fact! These days, bustards can be found wandering the semidesert plains of Africa, Australia, and Eurasia. Since they are partial to dry, warm climates, bustards in northern areas are migratory, heading south when the weather changes.

Bustards are medium and large birds, and they fly in typical crane fashion, head and neck straight out front, legs and feet trailing behind, and wings beating steadily. They often travel in flocks of a dozen or so, usually 200 or 300 feet above the ground.

Bustards sleep belly to the ground and head tucked between their shoulders. They almost never take a one-legged stance or perch on branches. Although they're strong fliers, they often escape predators on the run. Like cranes, they are omnivores who eat plants, herbs, grass, insects, snails, mice, and lizards. They also devour lots of locusts.

Bustards do *not* molt (the process by which all birds shed old feathers and replace them) all wing feathers at once, so they are still able to fly. Most birds molt on a yearly basis, and some do it twice a year.

Toe lockers. Why don't sleeping birds fall? Birds are equipped with grippy grabbers. Their feet have toes that "lock" in place when they squat on branches, wires, or other perches. The lock happens when muscles in the bird's upper legs pull attached tendons, which in turn tighten and lock their toes.

Feathers, like hairs, wear out, and birds molt or shed their plumes at least once a year, sometimes twice. Feathers are not shed all at once (except for penguins, ducks, and some other water birds). Most birds lose flight and tail feathers in pairs, so they are always able to fly!

Photo, facing page, courtesy Tom McHugh/Photo Researchers, Inc.

BIRDS

CRESTED AUKLET (*Aethia cristatella*)

The crested auklet, named for the nifty crest of a dozen or so black plumes on its forehead, hangs out in the North Pacific Ocean and on the islands of the Bering Sea. Seabirds of the far north, auklets and their relatives, the auks, murres, and puffins, belong to the family of birds known as alcids which occupy the ecological niche much like that of the penguins of the southern hemisphere. Like penguins, alcids are heavy-bodied swimmers, and their legs are placed far back on their bodies. They are clumsy clowns on land but graceful divers and swimmers. They feed by "flying" underwater in pursuit of fish. Unlike penguins, alcids are also strong fliers. They launch themselves from high cliffs and speed on the air currents.

Crested auklets are brownish black and gray with an orange bill, blue-black feet, and a wispy fringe of feathers behind each eye. They gather in great colonies (sometimes numbering thousands of birds) and nest in cliff crevices and between beached boulders.

How many contour feathers (the feathers that give a bird its shape) does a bird have? A sparrow may have more than 3,000, a hummingbird less than 1,000, and a swan more than 25,000.

Some birds have feathers on their feet which act as snowshoes in winter.

Photo, facing page, courtesy Kenneth W. Fink/Photo Researchers, Inc.

Pheasants fly only when absolutely necessary, but when they're in danger, they explode into flight. Capable of almost vertical flapping takeoffs, pheasants glide when airborne.

BULWER'S WATTLED PHEASANT (*Lophura bulweri*)

Bright blue, sickle-shaped wattles, a huge fan of white tail feathers, and the sound of rustling leaves are all tell-tale signs that the Bulwer's wattled pheasant is courting. To impress a potential mate, the male of this species goes through changes. Eyes like red Christmas lights, he struts with head lowered and feathers spread so that he looks a bit like a slow-moving satellite dish. As his tail feathers brush against the ground of the Asian forests where he lives, they shake dry leaves.

When it comes to birds-of-a-different-colored-feather, all pheasants tend to be alike—males and females are distinctly different colors. Male pheasants are some of the most spectacularly feathered birds in the avian kingdom, and many have long technicolored tail feathers. Males sport brighter plumage because they have the job of winning the female's attention. The females' duller plumage provides camouflage while she tends the nest.

The brilliant peacock is a pheasant.

Dirty bird! Dust baths are handy when birds want to scour parasites and dirt from feathers.

BIRDS

BLUE-CROWNED PIGEON (*Goura cristata*)

A lacy crown of blue-gray feathers gives crowned pigeons their name. These big birds feed on fallen fruit, seeds, berries, and insects, which they find in their home, the remote forests and swamps of New Guinea.

All pigeons are monogamous (they pick only one mate), and both sexes work together in nest-building, incubating, and brooding. Nests are stick platforms in trees, on the ground, or on cliff or building edges. Usually, there are two eggs per nest. The female is on duty for the night shift, while her mate takes over during the day. When they hatch, young pigeons have closed eyes and tiny pin-feathers. Both parents provide pigeon's milk. During incubation, the lining of the pigeon's crop (where food is softened for digestion) thickens and sheds. Pigeon's milk is the cheesy mixture that is then regurgitated. It sounds weird, but in food value, it's very similar to mammal's milk. To obtain food, young pigeons poke their small beaks inside their parent's throats. Later, the young are fed partially digested grains and seeds. Many species of pigeons rear two or more broods each year.

Passenger pigeons used to blacken the sky when they flew in flocks that numbered in the billions! They nested in colonies that sometimes covered a hundred miles, and tree branches broke from the weight of so many birds. But they were shot, trapped, and hunted by humans for their flesh. In 1914, passenger pigeons became extinct when Martha died in the Cincinnati Zoo.

Watch! When most birds drink, they tilt back their heads to swallow droplets. Pigeons, in contrast, suck water using their beaks like straws.

Birds like grouse, finches, and pigeons often need to escape danger. For acceleration, speed, and maneuverability, blunt, rounded wings are best.

Photo, facing page, courtesy Toni Angermayer/Photo Researchers, Inc.

GOMBESSA COELACANTH (*Latimeria chalumnae*)

How would you feel if you went fishing and pulled up a dinosaur in your net? Sound impossible? It is, since dinosaurs are extinct, but some animal species that lived 65 million years ago *are* still alive today. For instance, leatherback turtles and tuatara lizards are both very old species. So are some species of fish.

Not very long ago (in 1938), a captain of a South American fishing boat netted an extremely weird fish. The fish was a coelacanth (SEAL-ah-kanth), a species scientists had believed to be extinct for the last 80 million years or so. In fact, the real, live coelacanth was almost a fishy fossil. (It first appeared on Earth almost 400 million years ago.) Icthyologists (scientists who study fish) and others were very excited because this was a major scientific discovery.

Large, bony coelacanths belong to a group of fish named for the fleshy lobes at the base of their fins. Coelacanths grow to lengths of five feet, and they can swim backwards, upside down, and tails up! Because they have adapted to life in deep, deep water, coelacanths do not live long in captivity. Until scientists figure out a way to study them, they will remain mysterious fish.

Long before humans existed, extinctions were a fact of life. Dinosaurs ruled the Earth for more than 150 million years, but something happened 65 million years ago that wiped them out. Not only dinosaurs but winged pterosaurs, most large reptiles, many mammals, some birds and plants, and almost every kind of sea plankton disappeared. This was a mega-extinction! Was it caused by Earth's collision with an extraterrestrial force? No one knows for sure. Since humans and our ancestors have only existed for about 2 million years, we can only guess.

Loss of habitat (or living space), pollution, overhunting, and the introduction of new nonnative species (like sheep, rats, and cats) are four big threats to wild plants and animals.

ENDANGERED SPECIES

This native amphibian of Texas has a mating call that some say sounds like a tinkling bell.

HOUSTON TOAD (*Bufo houstonensis*)

Freckled, moist, warty, eyes bulging, the Houston toad looks just like a...well, a toad! To human eyes, toads and other amphibians aren't all that beautiful. But they are extremely important: they prey on pesky insects, and they also help control mosquito populations. And while toads are eating small critters, larger predators, like snakes, bats, and rodents, are eating toads.

Houston toads depend on year-round and part-time wetlands to survive. They spend much of their time in sandy ground where they can burrow down. But to reproduce, Houston toads need water. Clusters of 500 to 6,000 eggs are deposited in flooded fields, rain pools, and ponds. Within days, tiny tadpoles emerge from the eggs. The tadpoles need at least two months to metamorphose (change) into froglets. If puddles or ponds dry up too soon, the tadpoles—left high and dry—will die.

In the 1950s, drought killed many Houston toads. Since that time, the cities of Houston and Austin, home to the Houston toad, have grown so large that wetlands have been drained and covered over with houses. New roads and sewage lines have changed natural drainage patterns and dried up ponds.

Fortunately, concerned humans have created a nature preserve for the Houston toad, and the Houston Zoo has helped increase toad numbers with a breeding program. Captive-bred toads are turned loose in the preserve where they can live without harm from humans.

There's no denying the Houston toad is warty, but they're not the kind of warts that people get!

The International Union for Conservation of Nature has formed a special amphibian group as part of the Species Survival Commission to actively encourage amphibian conservation. Write: IUCN Species Survival Commission, C/O Chicago Zoological Society, Brookfield, IL 60503.

ENDANGERED SPECIES

GALÁPAGOS TORTOISE (*Geochelone* spp.)

Tortoises wandered the Earth even before the age of the dinosaurs. They are the most ancient of reptiles, dating back 250 million years. They haven't changed a whole lot since then, either.

If any tortoise looks as old and as wrinkled as time, it must be the giant of the Galápagos Islands off the coast of Ecuador. A full-grown Galápagos tortoise is 400 pounds of scaly, puckery skin, massive shell, and bowlegs. Tortoises are known for their amazing life span—sometimes as long as 150 years. But humans have made it difficult for tortoises to grow old.

In the 1800s, when the Galápagos Islands were discovered by European and American whaling vessels, sailors saw a great many tortoises. In fact, legends say a sailor could walk from island's end to end on the backs of the tortoises without touching the ground. The newly arrived humans killed tortoises for food. They also brought rats, cats, and dogs to the island, and those animals ate tortoise eggs and young turtles. Now, because their numbers have dwindled, Galápagos tortoises are an endangered species.

Turtles are the only reptiles with shells!

Another reptile, the American alligator, is a whole lot of help when it comes to keeping wetlands wet. These alligators create deep water holes and keep them free of weeds and muck. Even in the driest season, there's usually enough water left in these holes to keep turtles, fish, and snails alive. Some of these animals become food for mammals, birds, and alligators. But there are usually enough water-dependent animals left when the rains come to repopulate the wetland.

Some sea turtles, like the green sea turtle, *Chelonia mydas*, almost became extinct because humans valued its meat, eggs, and shell more than they valued the living creature. Although they are protected by law, green sea turtles will survive as a species only if humans stop killing them intentionally and accidentally in shrimp fishing nets.

ENDANGERED SPECIES

CALIFORNIA CONDOR (*Gymnogyps californianus*)

One of the biggest flying birds in the world, adult California condors sometimes weigh as much as 20 pounds, and their wings may span 10 feet when spread. They can reach an air speed of 60 miles per hour and travel 140 miles per day foraging for food. Condors have no feathers from the neck up, where their wrinkled skin is gray, yellow, red, and orange. Their body is black except for a white underwing, and their scaly claws are as big as a man's hand. No doubt about it, they look extremely weird to humans.

In the wild, a typical condor day starts with a few hours of grooming and preening while perched on a tree branch or other roosting site. By midmorning, the condor sweeps over the countryside in search of food. Condors are vultures, their hooked beaks made to tear apart carcasses, and like other scavengers, they help clean up the countryside by eating the flesh of dead animals.

California condors used to nest in caves and rocky crevices in very lonely cliffs near the Pacific coast of California. Fossil records tell us California condors date back 100,000 years, and at one time they feasted on the flesh of saber-toothed tigers and mastodons. Although they once thrived throughout what is now the American West, modern life has become deadly for these birds.

It's hard to prove exactly what has made the California condor an endangered species. Scientists know that condors have been killed by hunters, and some have died from head-on collisions with power lines. Also, because condors feed on carrion, whatever killed their prey—often poisons and pesticides—can kill them, too. For all these reasons, there were only about 60 wild California condors left by the 1960s. By 1980, there were less than 30. Finally, the last birds were caught and moved to sanctuaries. Captive breeding programs have increased the numbers, and projects for reintroducing condors to the wild are under way. Scientists hope that these birds will once again thrive in the American West.

California condors, eagles, and falcons are all *raptors*, diurnal (active during the day) birds of prey that feed mostly on the flesh of other animals.

Animals are us! What we do to animals, we do to ourselves. And we have only one planet to share.

You can help: Write letters to the president of the United States, members of Congress, your state governor, and your city's mayor. Let them know you support the Endangered Species Act, and tell them what you think should be done to save endangered wildlife.

Photo, facing page, courtesy Tom McHugh/Photo Researchers, Inc.

ENDANGERED SPECIES

HORNED GUAN (*Oreophasis derbianus*)

The horned guan wears a hat at all times. And an unusual hat, at that. The bright orangy red cap perched between the guan's eyes—and made of naked skin and bone—is in sharp contrast to the guan's glossy black body feathers.

Horned guan territory includes areas of southern Mexico all the way to Guatemala in South America. Although they do spend time on the ground, they are perfectly suited for life in trees. Horned guans build nests of twigs and leaves in the trees and bushes of mountain forests.

On the move, they jump and tiptoe along the thinnest and highest branches and then take off on long gliding flights, only flapping their wings when absolutely necessary.

When they are surprised, horned guans have a loud, throaty cry almost like an explosion. Forest intruders are greeted with a chatter of yellow beaks that resembles the sound of a Spanish dancer's castanets.

These birds love bean sprouts, and they also eat flowers, berries, mangoes, guavas, and seeds. Most of the time, they search for food in trees or bushes, and they might even be seen hanging upside down (hats wiggling) as they eat.

Like many birds, horned guans are endangered because forests are being cleared to make room for people.

Pop it! Helium balloons are popular items at fairs and parties because they float up, up, and away. But those balloons are deadly to birds, sea turtles, and other marine life who mistake them for edible jellyfish. The balloons can stick in the animal's throat and suffocate it.

Conservation has a history. As far back as 242 B.C., the Indian emperor, Ashoka, created nature preserves for animals. Kublai Khan (1215?-1294) banned the hunting of birds at certain times of the year. And Incan kings in South America had a death penalty for any human who killed a seabird.

ENDANGERED SPECIES

GIANT ARMADILLO (*Priodontes giganteus*)

Armored in a double layer of horn and bone, the giant armadillo looks as weird as its relatives, the sloth and the anteater. How does the armadillo develop its armor? A baby armadillo is born with tough, leathery skin that hardens into horny plates or bands as it grows. This armored shell is very handy for hiding from other animals. And because the plates are surrounded by flexible skin, armadillos of some species can roll up into a ball when they are threatened. That's good protection for an armadillo's very vulnerable belly, which is covered with soft skin and hair instead of scales.

Adult giant armadillos may measure more than 4½ feet from head to tail's end and weigh as much as 130 pounds. They live in the forests of South America east of the Andes, from central Venezuela to northeastern Argentina.

The armadillo's tongue is shaped like a worm, and it has many small bumps covered with sticky saliva. These sticky bumps are great for catching ants, worms, spiders, and insects. But the giant armadillo's favorite food treat is a mouthful of termites. Because giant armadillos have claws and powerful limbs, they are very good diggers and scratchers. They can tear up termite hills in search of food and leave holes so big a human can fit inside.

Giant armadillos are endangered because unfortunately their skins have been valued by humans for handbags, luggage, and belts. Also, much of their homeland is being developed by humans for farming and housing.

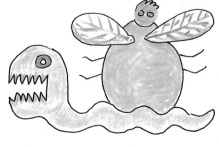

Termites are some of nature's best recyclers. They break down dead wood so it can go back into the earth. Without termites, the world would be smothered by dead plants. Termites are worldly critters, but they prefer tropical climates. Termite colonies build mounds up to 30 feet high out of dirt and saliva. Inside, each individual—worker, soldier, or queen—has a job to do.

Armadillo is a Spanish word referring to the armorlike coat of this critter.

/ANIMAL FREE

You can help: Don't buy cosmetics, jewelry, or leather goods that are made of wild animals! People who hunt wild animals commercially only do it because they can make money. If you're not sure what something is made of, or where it comes from, ask the salesperson.

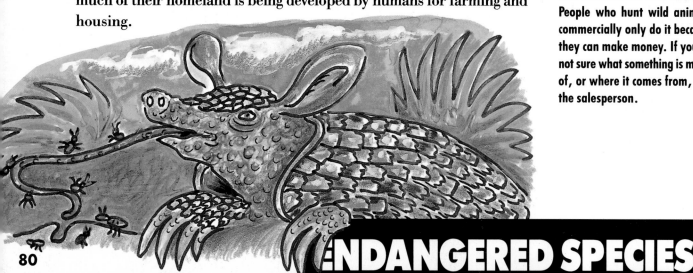

Photo, facing page, courtesy Paul Crum/Photo Researchers, Inc.

ENDANGERED SPECIES

FOSSA (*Cryptoprocta ferox*)

The fossa is a predator and the largest carnivore living in the warm, forested areas of Madagascar. Its body may grow to a length of 5 or 6 feet, and it has a sleek brown coat and a long, thin, graceful tail. Its face is marked with white eye patches topped with black triangles.

Fossas have retractile claws (like cats), and they are efficient hunters. They are also good climbers and quick runners. At night, they hunt lemurs and large birds, and their diet also includes frogs, lizards, and even insects.

The fossa lives *only* on Madagascar, the fourth largest island in the world. Madagascar is also the home of other animal species who live nowhere else. These species are very different from their relatives in other parts of the world because the island of Madagascar broke off from the mainland of Africa many millions of years ago and species evolved separately.

Because the fossa has been so heavily hunted by humans, it is listed as an endangered species. Also, most of the trees that at one time covered the island with rich, dense forests have been cut down by humans. As the forest disappears, so does the fossa and other endangered animals.

Although sometimes placed in the cat family, fossas walk on the soles of their feet like bears instead of walking on their toes like cats.

You can help: Trees need friends! To help keep the planet green: recycle paper; plant seedlings; join Tree Amigos. (*Amigos* means "friends" in Spanish.) Write: Center for Environmental Study, Tree Amigos Project, 143 Bostwick NE, Grand Rapids, MI 49503. Through Tree Amigos, you can adopt an acre of tropical rain forest or learn about other ways to help!

Introducing new species is a real threat for local wildlife. For instance, your own furry kitty cat is a deadly hunter of birds, lizards, frogs, and other wild animals. And the dingo, a wild dog, introduced to Australia by Aborigines, has helped drive native species to extinction.

SAUDI ARABIA

INDIAN OCEAN

SOUTH ATLANTIC OCEAN

AFRICA

MADAGASCAR

ENDANGERED SPECIES

MANED WOLF (*Chrysocyon brachyurus*)

From deep in the woodlands of central South America comes the cry, "Uaah uaah." Is it a bird? Is it a monkey? It might take you a long time to cry wolf—the maned wolf, that is.

The maned wolf, named for the thick dark mane along its back, is not closely related to other wolf species. Although it's about the same size as the true wolf (*Canis lupus*), its slender ears and sharp snout are more foxlike. The maned wolf travels alone except during mating season when pairs stay together.

Maned wolves are omnivorous, which means they eat plants *and* animals: fruits and nuts as well as rodents, birds, and even smaller animals. It's not unusual to see a maned wolf rooting for worms and snails among the leaves and grass of savannas and swamps. When they are hunting, maned wolves stop and start a lot. And they're always sniffing the air and wiggling their ears—the better to hear—as they search for prey.

When maned wolves play together, they charge full speed ahead and then leap into the air. This leaping ability comes in handy when they need to escape danger.

But humans are not easy to escape. Maned wolves are endangered by loss of habitat because people are clearing and burning the grasslands for farming. They are also hunted by people who fear the wolf will threaten domestic livestock.

Weird science! Scientists from the USSR decided to try to re-create the extinct mammoth by using a cell taken from a frozen bull in Siberia. They planned to implant the cell into an egg and uterus of a living female elephant. If it was done, the results have not been announced to the world.

Predators are animals that kill other animals for food. They are an important part of nature: their job is to keep their prey from having a population explosion.

ENDANGERED SPECIES

SPECTACLED BEAR (*Tremarctos ornatus*)

Named for the white patches of fur that often surround its eyes, the adult spectacled bear might look as if it's wearing goggles. This large, black bear lives in high mountain forests of western Venezuela, Colombia, Ecuador, Peru, and western Bolivia. It is a shy, solitary animal who lives alone or in small family groups.

Spectacled bears enjoy a good climb. These agile animals build stick platforms high in the branches of trees. The platforms give them easy access to their favorite foods—leaves, shoots, and fruit. In some areas of their range, they munch on young palm plants and cactus. Every now and then, they may prey on other wild animals, like llamas, or cattle.

These bears are nocturnal (active at night). During the day, they bed down in caves, on tree trunks, or under large shady trees.

Fewer and fewer spectacled bears survive these days as humans move into their territory. They are killed for their meat and their skins, and they are hunted for "sport."

No opera star! The spectacled bear has an extremely weird, shrill voice.

Bears were worshiped by Stone Age cave-dwellers. Our ancestors kept bear skulls on poles and danced around them.

Even 2,000 years ago, humans were a problem for bears. Ancient European tribes hunted bears for skins, and Roman emperors staged bloody fights between bears, dogs, and gladiators.

You can help: Join National Wildlife Federation. This is the nation's largest conservation organization. For more than 50 years, NWF has worked to conserve wildlife and its habitat. NWF was instrumental in obtaining enactment of the Endangered Species Act in 1973 and has continued working to defend and strengthen that important environmental law. Write: NWF, 1400 16th Street, N.W., Washington, D.C. 20036.

ENDANGERED SPECIES

MARKHOR (*Capra falconeri*)

Markhors are wild goats with a twist. Their great horns grow in a pattern that seems a bit screwy —corkscrewy. Adult males use these horns to battle with each other to test who's strongest. When they are fighting, they turn their heads side to side so their horns clash like swords, and sometimes they rear up on their hind legs. Markhors also sport bushy beards, long hair, and thick manes. One of the largest species of goats, they can grow to a height of 100 centimeters (more than 3 feet).

Adapted for life at high altitudes where the air is thin and cold, these animals graze the rocky slopes of Asiatic mountains. They become active in the afternoon and evening when they search for grass, weeds, leaves, twigs, and shrubs.

Wild markhors breed from late summer to midwinter. Females usually give birth to one or two energetic kids. Mothers protect their young by fighting off intruders with their horns or by acting as a decoy for predators.

Markhors are threatened by loss of living space because of competition from humans and domestic livestock. They are also hunted for meat and their horns taken as trophies.

The markhor is an even-toed ungulate. That may sound like something squishy, but it really means a hoofed mammal with an even number of toes.

Great Grinders! A goat is an herbivore (plant eater) with no front teeth. It pulls its food with sturdy lips, tongue, tough upper gums, and small lower teeth. A goat's jaw moves front to back and side to side.

Some animals known only by their fossils were hunted to extinction by our early ancestors. The sivatherium was a close relative of the giraffe. And the 12-foot-tall marsupial named Palorchestes had a trunk, claws, and a long tail and looked extremely weird.

ENDANGERED SPECIES

GREAT INDIAN ONE-HORNED RHINOCEROS (*Rhinoceros unicornis*)

Reaching a length of 13 feet, a shoulder height of 6 feet, and a weight of 2 tons, the great Indian one-horned rhinoceros doesn't look easy to push around. But this giant, now living only in a few areas of Nepal and eastern India, has been hunted almost to extinction mostly because of its one and only horn.

What's in a horn? Actually, a rhinoceros horn is made of hairlike growths. If you put it under a microscope, you wouldn't see individual hairs: rhino horns and hair are both made of keratin, a fibrous protein. For centuries, many Asian people have believed that rhino horn powder is strong medicine. And jewelry and daggers made of rhino horn are thought to bring human owners power. These traditions have taken a terrible toll on the rhinoceros. Poachers may earn more than $1,000 for each rhino horn, and in some places, that's more money than the average worker would make in two years. With profits like this, hunting continues even though it's against the law. So, one thing to do is to eliminate the demand for these "products."

Illegal hunting endangers *many* animals besides the rhinoceros. Great blue whales, cheetahs, African elephants, and mountain gorillas are all the victims of overhunting.

There are five species of rhinoceroses still living on earth. Two species have a single horn, like the Indian rhinoceros. The other three species have two horns growing in a row, one right after the other.

You won't mistake the great Indian rhinoceros for its relatives in Africa because its skin, which has lots of loose folds, resembles a giant suit of armor. African rhinos, in contrast, are fairly fold-free.

Photo, facing page, courtesy S. Nagendra/Photo Researchers, Inc.

African elephants are illegally hunted for their ivory tusks. A tusk is a great tooth that keeps on growing and growing. The average elephant will produce about half a ton of ivory in a lifetime.

ENDANGERED SPECIES

WEST INDIAN MANATEE (*Trichechus manatus*)

Chubby, neckless, wrinkly, and tuskless, the gentle mammals known as manatees spend much of their time munching on sea vegetables in shallow ocean waters. In fact, a grown-up manatee can devour 100 pounds of plants each day. Although they may weigh as much as 3,500 pounds and grow longer than 12 feet, these aquatic mammals are very graceful swimmers. Propelled by spoon-shaped tails and flippered forelimbs, manatees slowly graze coastal waters, sometimes cruising 150 miles in one summer.

Manatees seem to occupy most of their day eating and playing—they trade gentle kisses, nibbles, and caresses—in warm waters. And sometimes, they will bob up to a boat to be petted. In the United States, where they are protected by the Endangered Species Act, their only enemies are human vandals and power boats. Because they live along the shores and rivers of Florida and Caribbean islands, manatees are in constant danger of injury or death from speeding motorboats. Most living manatees encountered by scientists have many scars from boat collisions. Humans can help manatees by treating them with respect and slowing down their boats, or, better yet, by avoiding waters in which manatees live.

Scoop the loop! Plastic loops that ring six-pack cans get tossed out with the garbage and often end up floating in our planet's oceans. When loops get caught around the necks of baby birds, seals, otters, and other animals, they are deadly. If you find loop litter, make sure the plastic gets cut up into tiny pieces so it can't harm another animal.

Manatees belong to the class Sirenia. Sailors on long, long voyages have been known to mistake swimming manatees for mermaids and singing sirens.

Manatees are relatives of elephants, and they have been swimming in Earth's oceans for more than 45 million years.

ENDANGERED SPECIES

HUMPBACK WHALE (*Megaptera novaeangliae*)

What weighs 45 tons, sings, is 50 feet long, and is very, very smart? If you guessed a humpback whale, you're smart, too. Some scientists consider whales among the smartest living creatures on Earth.

Humpbacks travel from feeding grounds in cold polar waters all the way to breeding grounds in warmer, tropical waters. They are fairly slow swimmers, reaching top speeds of just 11 miles per hour. These giant mammals swim behind schools of fish so they can eat an ocean smorgasbord of crustaceans, mackerel, cod, salmon, herring, and krill (tiny shrimplike crustaceans), which is strained from the water through fringed plates in the whale's mouth. These strainers are called baleen.

Humpbacks are known for their songs. They moan, grunt, groan, snore, squeal, and chirrup. And not just any old way! Each whale has its own tunes that it can sing again and again.

The biggest problem for humpback whales is us. Since the early days of whaling, thousands of whales have been killed. Their blubber has been used for gelatin, margarine, lamp oil, and glue. These days, other products like petroleum take the place of whale blubber. Since 1966, humpbacks have been protected from hunting except in a few cases. Still, the humpback population has recovered slowly. One reason is because adult whale females (cows) usually give birth to just one calf every two or three years. And now, because so many people want to see whales up close, scientists are studying how tourism may be adversely affecting these singing giants.

Pollution is a major threat to wildlife. Toxic waste from a city in the U.S. can pollute land, rivers, and oceans around the world with the help of wind and rain. We humans need to clean up our act!

Ocean olympics! Whales are nature's high-jumpers. They are capable of 20-foot leaps in the air.

Besides the humpback whales, seven other species of whales are on the federal Endangered Species list.

Photo, facing page, courtesy Francois Gohier/Photo Researchers, Inc.

ENDANGERED SPECIES

ORANGUTAN (*Pongo pygmaeus*)

Orangutans belong to the group known as great apes. So do chimpanzees and gorillas. Because of their anatomy and their brain power, they are the most humanlike of all non-human animals. In fact, they are our closest relatives. Among this group, the big orange orangutan is the only tree-dwelling ape.

Gazing at the world through woeful eyes, orangutans live quietly in the trees of rain forests in Borneo and Sumatra. They are hefty—adult males may weigh 200 pounds and females about 90—and strong and covered with shaggy hair. When it's standing, an orangutan's arms can reach its ankles, and some have an 8-foot arm spread! It's hard to believe these primates blend in with their surroundings, but they are very hard to spot hanging out in tree branches.

Orangutans have social relationships much like other apes, although adult males lead very solitary lives. Adult females form "friendships," and adolescents (like human teenagers) hang out together.

Orang moms are very careful mothers. They nurse, cuddle, and wash their babies with rainwater. Like human infants, baby orangutans cry when they are cold or hungry.

In the Malayan language, the word *orang-utan* means "forest man." Orangutans are creatures of the jungle, where their only enemy is man. They are protected by law, but they are still in danger of becoming extinct. Like other primates, much of their habitat is disappearing through human activities like farming and logging. Human poachers also kidnap young orangutans and sell them illegally to private collectors.

All nonhuman primates need our help if their offspring are going to survive in the future. In fact, all plants and animals need human friends who will strive to ensure a healthy world for all of us to share.

All the great apes need our help! There are very few mountain gorillas left, and chimpanzees and pygmy chimpanzees (our closest primate relatives) are disappearing quickly.

BIG BRAIN

FLEXIBLE

It takes a big brain to be a primate. To qualify, you must have flexible hands (with grasping fingers) and a history of living in trees. Monkeys, apes, and prosimians are all primates. We humans are primates, too!

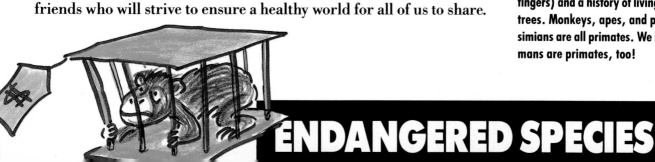

ENDANGERED SPECIES

Photo, facing page,
courtesy Tom McHugh/Photo Researchers, Inc.

Beaky Smile!

Spiny-tooth Parrot Fish (Family: Scaridae)

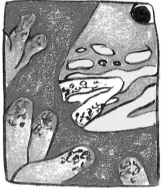

Complete with a very toothy beak, colorful parrot fishes are well equipped to scrape algae from coral reefs in tropical seas around the world. Parrot fishes are herbivores (animal who feed only on plants), but they often take bites of coral along with algae. They use toothlike plates in the back of their throat to crush and grind each tough mouthful. They digest what's usable and expel the rest, and their droppings create calcified piles of white coral sand.

Parrot fishes are steady swimmers, and their caudal (tail) fin is made for cruising (it even works for a quick getaway from predators). Although they do not usually travel in schools, they are sometimes called "cattle of the sea." That's because parrot fishes have a strong homing instinct, and groups can be seen heading toward special feeding grounds as the tides go in or out.

Some parrot fishes have an unusual sleeping habit. As night falls, the fish begins to secrete a thick mucous that surrounds its body like a sleeping bag. The process takes about thirty minutes to complete. The mucous sac helps protect the parrot fish from nocturnal (nighttime) predators like the moray eel. In the morning, the fish struggles to emerge from its sac (this also takes about 30 minutes) and begins its search for food.

There are more than 75 species of parrot fishes, all of them colorful. Parrot fishes of some species change colors two or more times as they mature in a lifetime, and males and females may or may not be the same color. The spiny-tooth parrot fish is not as beaky as its relatives. True to its name, it's toothy!

School's out! Many species of fishes swim together in groups called schools. Fishes may school together to breed, to feed, or for safety in numbers because predators find large schools confusing. Ichthyologists have learned that schooling fishes use body coloring and water vibrations to stay together with their neighbors.

Parrot fishes use their beaky teeth to bite off chunks of coral reef with each mouthful of algae. Coral looks like a rock, right? Actually, it is made of skeletons! There's nothing spooky about it because the skeletons belonged to microscopic sea creatures.

In the sink! Swim bladders keep many fishes from sinking to the bottom even though they are heavier than seawater. This gas-filled chamber allows a fish to increase its volume without adding to its weight. A fish deflates its bladder to lower its body and inflates it to rise.

Photo, facing page, courtesy Scott Johnson/Photo Researchers, Inc.

FISHES

Out of more than 20,000 fish species worldwide, only about 50 are poisonous. Stingrays, stonefishes, and lionfishes are among those that can cause painful problems for humans. But poisonous fishes mostly use their venom as a defense against large fish predators.

Stonefish (*Synanceia verrucosa*)

The warty, blobby, blotchy stonefish can be deadly. In fact, it has the most poisonous venom of all fishes! The spines of its dorsal fin (located on its back) are as sharp as hypodermic needles, and they are made for injecting poison. Skin divers must be especially careful because a stonefish is hard to spot. All those warts and blobs on the fish's skin provide camouflage; waiting for unsuspecting prey to swim by, a stonefish looks much like a rock or stone on the ocean bottom. If an unlucky swimmer steps on a stonefish, the pressure of his body weight will cause venom glands (located near the base of the dorsal fin spines) to inject poison into his foot. Stonefish poison has been known to kill a human within two hours of injection!

There are ten species of stonefish; most live in tropical seas where they prefer rocky bottom areas. This particular stonefish lives in Indo-Pacific waters. Some ichthyologists (ick-thee-OL-oh-gists), scientists who study fishes, believe stonefishes are related to scorpionfishes, while other scientists group stonefishes in their very own family: Synanceiidae.

Fishy feelies! Landlubbers have nothing to compare with a fish's lateral line. These sensory receptors lining the body of many fishes detect any change in surrounding water pressure, direction, or flow, as well as low-frequency sound.

Stingrays—named for the poisonous sting of their whip-thin tail—may weigh more than 500 pounds (almost 300 kg) and have a wingspan greater than 10 feet (3 m). These giants hang out on sandy ocean bottoms and cruise in search of crustaceans and fishes to eat.

Photo, facing page, courtesy Steinhart Aquarium/Photo Researchers, Inc.

F I S H E S

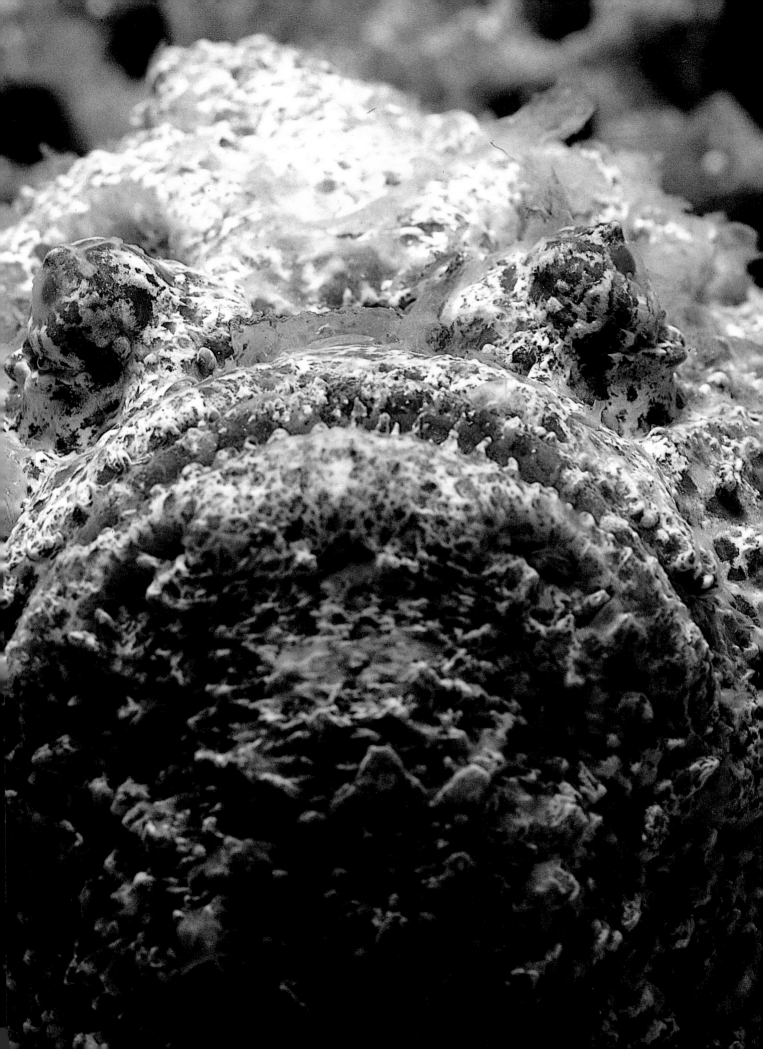

A Pop-eyed Hop and a Skip!

Stranded at low tide, some water-only fishes use their pectoral (chest) fins to push themselves off bare rocks and back into the ocean.

Mudskipper (*Periophthalmus barbarus*)

At low tide among the mangroves in the muddy swamps of Africa, Southeast Asia, and Australasia, you'll find mudskippers hopping and "skipping" about like frogs—out of water! Their bulging eyes rise like mini headlamps from their large heads, giving them an even froggier look. Pectoral fins act as legs while long fishy tails trail behind. They can move so quickly that icthyologists are left in the mud. Mudskippers spend most of their air time searching for insects to eat, or they might be on the lookout for a mate or even chasing away other mudskippers.

Since a mudskipper is a fish, how does it breathe air? Easily, because it is equipped with an aqualung of sorts, which is actually water caught inside its gill chambers. For extra breathing power, it also absorbs oxygen through the skin of its throat and mouth.

Mudskippers aren't the only fishes that can breathe air. Three hundred-million-year-old lungfishes have both gills *and* lungs. They can gulp air into their mouths! Some lungfishes bury themselves in the earth during times of drought and wait for rain.

Mudskippers belong to a group of fishes called gobies. Of about 2,000 species of gobies, only a few can spend time out of water and survive.

When they are on land, mudskippers keep their pop-eyes wet by rolling them around in their sockets! Their eyes are also covered with a clear layer of very thick skin.

Speedy slime! The scales of most fishes are slimy for two reasons: slime is a lubricant, which makes it easier for a fish to move through water with less friction; slime seals a fish and makes it watertight. Without slime, ocean fish would soak up so much salt from the sea they would be poisoned.

Photo, facing page, courtesy Zig Leszczynski/Photo Researchers, Inc.

Monster from the Deep

Panamic Green Moray (*Gymnothorax castaneus*)

Razor-sharp teeth in a gaping mouth, leathery skin that is scaleless and wrinkled, and a long snakelike body make the Panamic green moray a fish you want to avoid. These fishes prefer to lurk in rocky caves and coral crevices waiting for fish and other prey to swim by (sometimes at night they'll slither into deep water in search of food). All it takes is a forward thrust of the head, a snap of the jaw, and the satisfied moray coils back into its lair to wait for more food.

Although morays are fierce predators, they don't scare everybody. Some species of shrimp work as moray "cleaners." They crawl all around the moray's head (they even climb inside its toothy mouth!) removing parasites and scraps of food, and the moray never harms them.

Green morays get their name from the yellow slime covering their blue body: the result is a weird brownish-green color. Most green morays are less than 5 feet long, but a few reach a length of 10 feet!

The Panamic green moray lives in warm waters of North and South America. There are more than 110 species of morays, including the zebra, the spotted, and the dragon, living in tropical and subtropical waters. Morays are known for a sharp sense of smell (the better to sniff food) and a short temper when provoked. Skin divers have died from infection after receiving a deep, poisonous bite from an irritated moray. But morays attack only when threatened, and most of the time, they would rather hide than fight.

Big mouth! Some species of morays have such big mouths they can't close them.

For Ancient Romans, a pool filled with moray eels was a sign of wealth and good eats.

Mythical beast? Oarfishes are long snakelike fishes that resemble true eels. They reach a length of more than 10 feet (and according to unauthenticated reports, 20 feet!) and cruise the oceans. Oarfishes may be the mythical sea creatures that sailors have told of for centuries.

"Elvers" are baby eels, not elves.

Photo, facing page, courtesy Mike Neumann/Photo Researchers, Inc.

FISHES

Pregnant Pops!

Australian Sea Horse (*Hippocampus breviceps*)

When does a Pop become a Mom? When he's a sea horse, of course. Male sea horses really do become pregnant! But first, they must meet females and play the mating game.

Courtship begins at dawn, and it is colorful. Both males and females display bright colors—pinks and oranges—to let others know they're available. The male also fills his special abdominal pouch with water. When a pair meets, they wrap their prehensile (grasping) tails around a comfortable holdfast and begin to circle like horses on a carousel.

Soon, the male is ready to receive the female's eggs. In preparation, he begins to jacknife his body while pumping water in and out of his pouch (the same movement the male will use later to release young sea horses at birth). This is the signal for the female to place her ovipositor (egg-laying tube) inside the opening of the male's pouch. There, the eggs are fertilized by his sperm, and the female's job is finished. It is up to Pop to protect, care for, and nourish the developing embryos for the next few weeks until birth. Labor can take a few hours or even days.

Sea horses are special in other ways, too. Each of their two eyes work independently—all the better to spy small crustaceans and other prey to ambush. A quick, strong, suck of the sea horse's snout disposes of a meal, which they digest without the help of teeth or stomach. How? Even icthyologists aren't sure!

Sea horses move with the help of their single dorsal fin, and they also have two teensy pectoral fins for steering and balance. They are the world's slooowwwest fish, moving less than one foot per minute. That speed wouldn't win any horse races!

There are about 35 species of sea horses living in shallow coastal seas all the way from Tasmania in the south to the English Channel in the north. They range in length from the half-inch New Caledonian sea horse to the 14-inch Eastern Pacific sea horse. This fish family also includes seadragons and pipefishes.

What fish has a horse's head, a monkey's tail, and a pouch like a kangaroo? A male sea horse, of course!

How do we know the pregnant "Pop" isn't really a "Mom"? Icthyologists have proven that male sea horses produce sperm like all male animals, and females produce eggs.

Ancient Romans believed sea horses could help cure baldness when their ashes were applied to the head. These days, we know you would have better luck with a toupee!

Photo, facing page, courtesy Paul A. Zahl/Photo Researchers, Inc.

F I S H E S

Bubble Double

Bubble-eye Goldfish (*Carassius auratus*)

Not all goldfish are gold! In fact, some have red caps and pink eyes, others sport black, red, and white spots, and there are even silvery black-scaled goldfish. How did they get that way?

According to Chinese legend, there was a great drought almost 3,000 years ago (769 B.C.) when no rain fell for 100 days. To appease the gods, the farmers made sacrificial gifts to the dry ponds, and, suddenly, a burbling brook splashed out of the ground—filled with tiny gold fishes! And at just that very moment, the rains began to fall.

Even if the legend isn't true, for centuries, people in Asia have been raising goldfishes. In about 960, a Chinese governor of the Sung dynasty created a beautiful goldfish pond, and there was once a harsh penalty for anyone who tried to kill and eat the fish for food. By 1136, there were historical reports that people were breeding goldfishes artificially, some of which turned into extremely, extremely weird fishes!

Goldfishes, carp, and minnows all belong to the same family. Wild goldfishes (a.k.a. Johnny carp, Missouri minnow, and crucian carp) are a dull brown color and a basic fish shape. They are also the ancestors of all exotic goldfishes! Only after breeders begin pairing and mating fishes with special qualities do exotic breeds like the bubble-eye goldfish appear! If exotic goldfishes are allowed to breed naturally, their offspring eventually regain the plain-John look of a Johnny carp.

Tiny or tall? Goldfish grow as large as their surroundings allow. In a small aquarium, they will enlarge just a few inches, but placed in a pond, they begin to grow and grow and grow—sometimes as much as 18 inches!

A healthy goldfish can live for twenty years when it is well cared for!

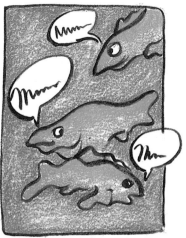

Goldfish have good hearing and often "murmur" among themselves, and they can easily be trained to respond to the sound of a bell.

FISHES

Spotted Wobbegong Australian Carpet Shark (*Orectolobus maculatus*)

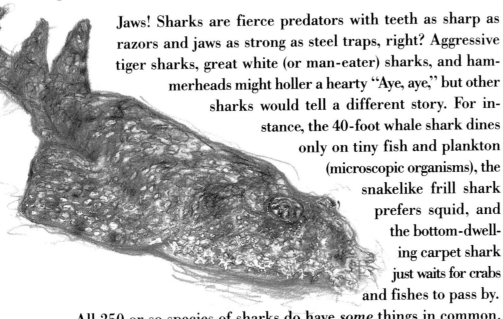

Jaws! Sharks are fierce predators with teeth as sharp as razors and jaws as strong as steel traps, right? Aggressive tiger sharks, great white (or man-eater) sharks, and hammerheads might holler a hearty "Aye, aye," but other sharks would tell a different story. For instance, the 40-foot whale shark dines only on tiny fish and plankton (microscopic organisms), the snakelike frill shark prefers squid, and the bottom-dwelling carpet shark just waits for crabs and fishes to pass by.

All 250 or so species of sharks do have *some* things in common. They (and their relatives, rays and skates) are known for their well-developed lower jaws and bony teeth as well as their skeletons, which are made of cartilage instead of bone. The cartilage is hard, not rubbery, and that is one reason many sharks have such powerful bites. Sharks have several rows of teeth and two nostrils that do not open into their mouth. Their scales are toothlike in structure. And, of course, they have dorsal fins! They are mostly marine fish, although a few species will travel up freshwater rivers.

The spotted wobbegong is a carpet shark that lives off the coast of Australia and other tropical Indonesian and Pacific waters. It is a carnivore (flesh-eater) and prefers small fish and crabs. Like all sharks, it is extra-weird looking! It boasts a broad snout fringed with feathery, weedy-looking barbels. Its bumpy brownish body is mottled with lots of eyespots (spots that look like eyes), which provide camouflage and a rocklike appearance on the ocean floor.

The "yikes" bite! Sharks have many rows of teeth, and the outer ones are always replaced by inner ones.

Size it up. The world's largest fish, the whale shark, reaches a length of almost 50 feet (about 15 m) and weighs in at 20 tons! The teensiest fish is the 0.3-inch-long (8 mm) dwarf pygmy goby.

Speedy ocean swimmers such as sharks, tuna, and rays have no swim bladder. These fish will sink slowly whenever they stop swimming. For this reason, they are *always* on the move.

Photo, facing page, courtesy Tom McHugh/Photo Researchers, Inc.

Lots of Lip

Spotfin Jawfish (*Opistognathus macrognathus*)

It's no surprise that a fish known as the jawfish has a big head and plenty of jawbone. In fact, the spotfin jawfish can open its mouth wide enough to eat a fish that is larger than its own head! But jawfishes use their mouths for other purposes.

Some male jawfishes incubate their young by the mouthful. Eggs are carried orally until the young hatch and are ready to swim on their own. Even then, the fry (young fishes) stay very close to their parents and swim for cover (sometimes inside their parent's mouth) whenever danger threatens.

Although jawfishes look fierce, they only reach a length of 6 inches or less. For safety and shelter, some species make holes in the sand and adorn the entrance with pebbles, shells, and bits of coral. They enter tail first at the first sign of danger and peer out to see if all is clear.

Jawfishes swim in the warm waters of the Atlantic Ocean, the Gulf of Mexico, the Caribbean, the Indian Ocean, and the Gulf of California region.

A mouthful! This male jawfish has a mouth filled with eggs. It is his job to incubate the eggs until they hatch.

When it comes to reproduction, fishes are a varied group. Many species release their eggs into water where they are fertilized and develop on their own. Others, like the jawfish, incubate eggs in their mouth. Still others, sharks, for instance, give birth to live young. Skates and rays, in contrast, lay already fertilized eggs inside egg cases (sometimes known as a "mermaid's purse") that attach to seaweed.

Photo, facing page, courtesy Fred McConnaughey/Photo Researchers, Inc.

No Bones About It!

Breathing easy! Primitive fishes (those most like their fish ancestors) have two ways to breathe—through gills *and* lungs.

Pacific Hagfish (*Eptatretus stouti*)

Wormy and *extremely* slimy, Pacific hagfishes are the ugliest of the uglies! Hags are also the most primitive of all fishes, which means they are simplest in structure. They are jawless fishes, eellike in shape, with a skeleton made of cartilage instead of bone. Their skin is scaleless as well as slippery. When they are distressed, hags secrete lots of slime from mucous glands in their reddish, gray-brown skin. They have one nostril (which they use to find prey), but their eyes are not visible, and they're blind.

Hagfishes are scavengers and spend their lives imbedded in soft muddy ocean bottoms where the water is cold and deep. Only their snouts can be seen. They emerge after dark to feed on dead or injured fishes—how hags eat is even weirder than how they look—from the *inside out*. They penetrate the skin of another fish by boring a hole with their raspy tongue. Once they have a grip with their triangular lips, they eat out the intestines first and then the flesh, leaving only skin and bones.

Pacific hagfishes live off the coast of North America. Other species of hagfish live in almost all parts of the world—in the North Atlantic Ocean, the Mediterranean Sea, the Sea of Japan, and off the coasts of South Africa and South America.

Why don't bony fish roll over? Deep bodies, much like a sailboat's keel, and dorsal fins keep bony fishes from keeling over.

Hagfishes grow to a length of two extremely weird feet.

Photo, facing page, courtesy Steinhart Aquarium/Photo Researchers, Inc.

F I S H E S

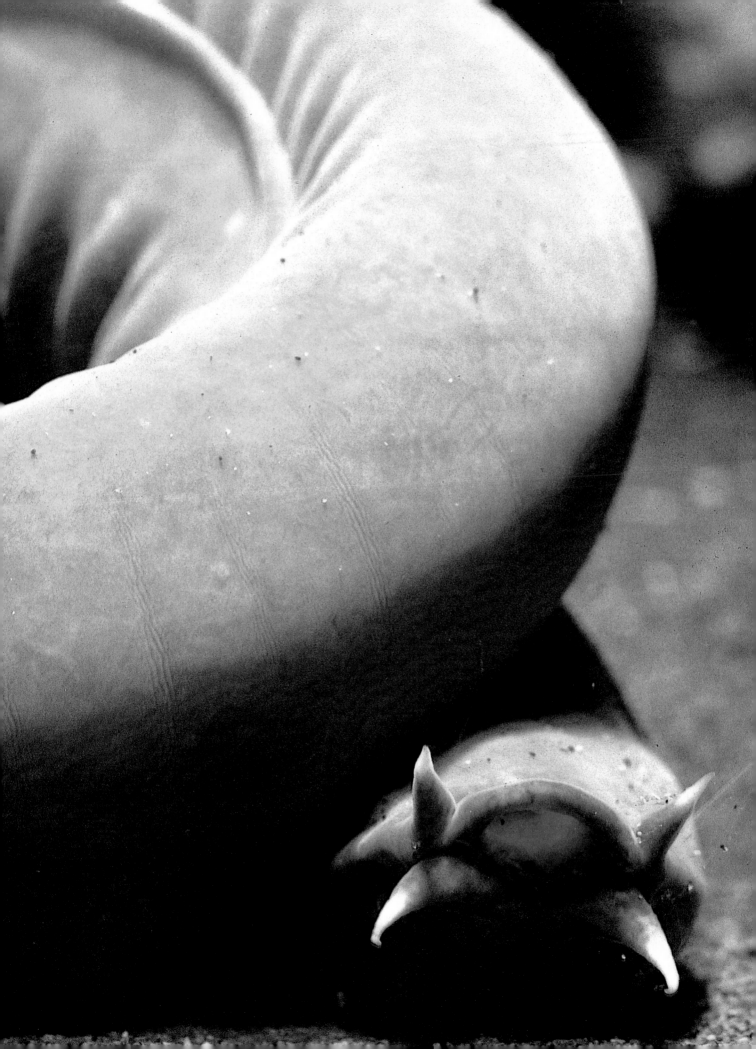

Walking Catfish (*Clarias batrachus*)

Walking catfishes can walk about on land using their pectoral leglike fins and moving with a snakelike slither. Of course, that's not all it takes for these fishes to walk on land!

Walking catfishes have an extra-special lunglike breathing apparatus tucked in front of their gills and reaching along both sides of the spine like many roots well supplied with blood. This makes it possible for them to breathe air and stay out of water on rainy nights for as long as several hours. To make room for these extra "lungs," the front of their body is thick. Walking catfishes have a thin, flat tail, and their skin is covered with mucous for protection from the dry air.

These fishes grow to a length of 16 inches, and they are hardy. That hardiness has proved a problem for other fishes. Walking catfishes are native to Southeast Asia, but they have been imported by fish hobbyists to Guam, the Hawaiian Islands, and Florida where they were set free, escaped, or just walked away. Now they are thriving in their new homes, and they are threatening native species. Walking catfishes are extremely aggressive and will attack and eat almost any other fish—even if it's bigger than they are!

When they are in the swim, walking catfishes prefer slow-moving, dirty water. If the pond or their food supply dries up, they simply walk to new territory.

Pleased to meet you, now move over, buster! Just like walking catfish, many other plant and animal species have caused problems for native wildlife when they were introduced by humans. The wild dingo in Australia killed many animals that were there long before it arrived. Rats (brought by sailors) destroyed much of the tortoise population of the Galápagos Islands. And house cats are deadly predators of song birds and other wildlife in the United States and Europe.

Photo, facing page, courtesy Photo Researchers, Inc.

FISHES

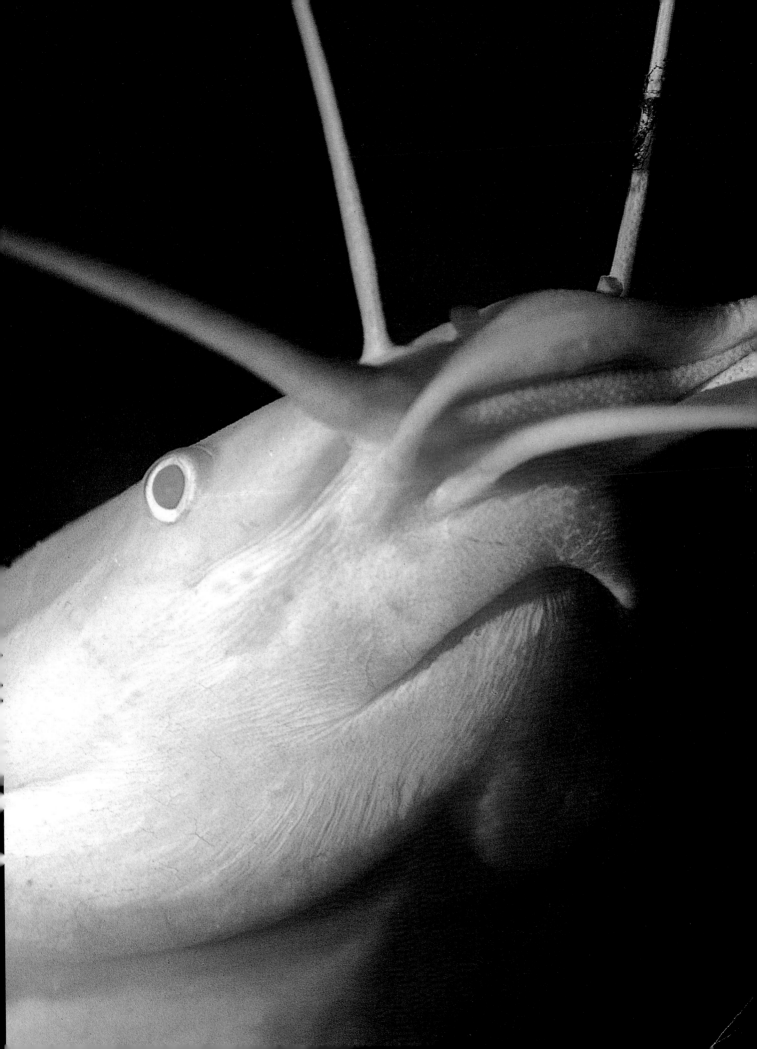

C-O Sole (*Pleuronichthys coenosis*)

There are more than 500 species of flatfish—fishes that swim flat against the bottom of the sea. But how did they get that way? They weren't born flat! Newly hatched flatfishes look like most larval fishes: they're small, and they swim upright. But just weeks later, drastic changes take place. Their bodies become flatter and flatter, and the eye on one side of their head slowly moves over the top to join the other eye. The blind side is now the downside, and the side with two eyes is on top. To make appearances even odder, the skull and the mouth also twist upward. Finally, flatfishes sink to the ocean bottom, where they stay for the rest of their very flat lives.

Depending on which side the eyes settle, flatfishes are known as "left-eyed" or "right-eyed." Members of the scientific family Bothidae—various flounders, sole, whiffs, halibuts, and sanddabs—are left-eyed. In contrast, members of the scientific family Pleuronectidae—some flounders, turbots, sole, and plaice—are right-eyed. The C-O sole, a right-eyed flounder, prefers warm seas worldwide.

Brazilian hiccup fish gulp air that sounds like a hiccup when released. The loudest hiccups can be heard as far away as a mile!

Turn signals. Fishes use their fins for balance, propulsion, braking, and steering. This fish looks as if it's about to make a right turn, but actually, it uses the right fin to turn to the left.

Small fry! Newly hatched fish are known as "fry."

Photo, facing page, courtesy Tom McHugh/Photo Researchers, Inc.

FISHES

Spit It Out!

Red Devil Cichlid (*Cichlasoma labiatum*)

Splashy, rainbow-colored cichlids (like the red devil) live in tropical freshwater streams and lakes of North, Central, and South America, as well as Africa and India. A few robust species survive in salty or coastal areas. There are about 600 species in all.

Cichlids are aggressive carnivores that eat the flesh of other fish *and* small animals. But cichlid parents are attentive and careful: both males and females provide care and schooling for their offspring. While young cichlids are still under the watchful eye of grown-ups, they must stay in school, which means they stay together. If a single young cichlid tries to swim solo, a parent may grasp it by mouth and spit it back into the group.

Some species of cichlids are mouthbrooders, which means the female carries the eggs in her mouth. After the eggs hatch, the larvae remain in their mother's mouth for several days until they can swim on their own. Even then, they return to Mom when danger threatens. Cichlid species who are not mouthbrooders deposit their eggs on water plants, stones, and pieces of wood. When the young are newly hatched, their parents move them into a "nursery" dug in the sandy river or lake bottom.

Some mouthbrooding parents blow or spit their fry from their mouth when they are ready to feed. That way, the young can learn to feed, too. Fry return to the mouth when danger threatens or night falls.

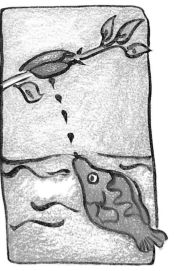

Another fish with spit is the archer fish of India and Australasia. This swamp-dwelling creature takes aim and squirts a stream of water above the water's surface to hit spiders and insects as far away as five feet (1.5 m).

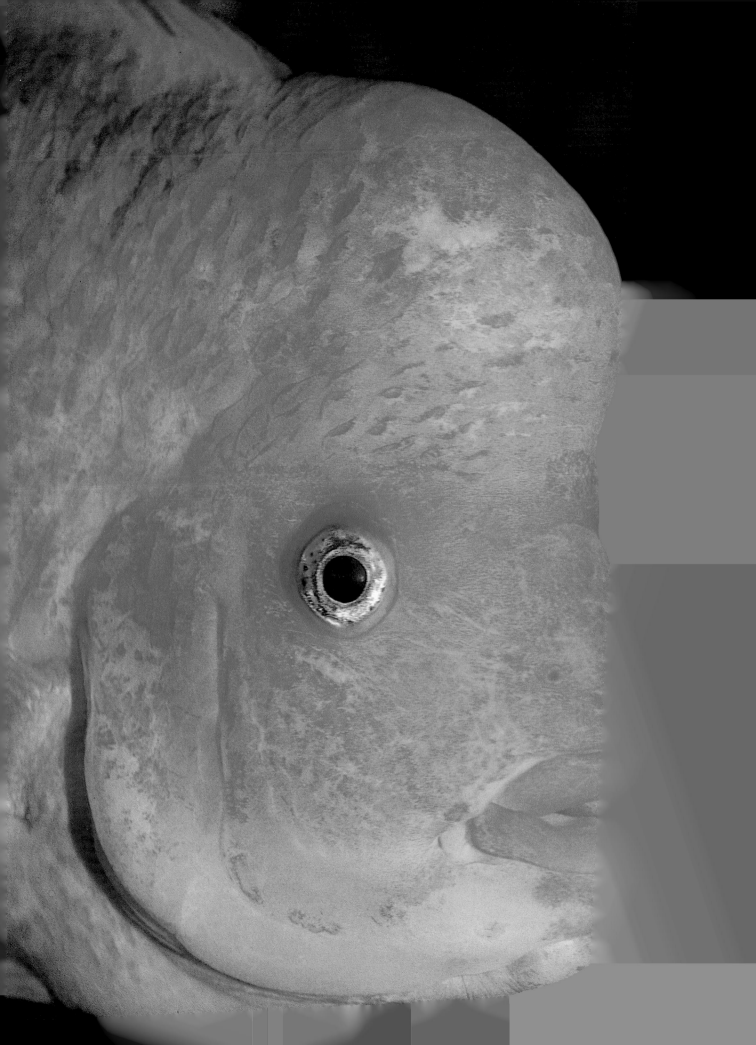

Z-Z-Z-Z-Zap!

The electric eel of the Amazon uses electroplates in its muscles to deliver 500-volt shocks that can kill small prey.

Elephant-nosed Fish (*Gnathonemus numenius*)

Elephant-nosed fish are shocking! At least, like many species of fish, their bodies produce electrical currents. Some fish, electric eels and electric catfishes, for instance, use their shocks to stun and kill prey. Elephant-nosed fish, in contrast, use their mild electrical abilities as a sort of radar to track food. Electrical currents are produced by specially modified muscles on both sides of the tail.

The elephant-nosed fish has a snout to shout about, but this snout is really a mouth! It is used to probe for food on muddy bottoms of African rivers, streams, and lakes where they live. Because an elephant-nosed fish has such a small mouth and very few teeth, it dines on small aquatic invertebrates such as insects, various larvae, and worms.

There are more than 100 species of these fish, and they all have a miniature elephant-sized mouth. They vary in length from 6 inches to 5 feet. They are active at night and hide from daylight.

Electric catfish deliver 100 volts of electricity. That's enough to stun and kill small fish. They also use it as underwater sonar to locate prey. Electric organs in the catfish are located in glandular cells in the skin instead of muscles.

Nothing fishy! Whales, dolphins, and porpoises are marine mammals, not fishes. Their tails (flukes) are horizontal and move up and down. Fishes, in contrast, have vertical tail (caudal) fins that move side to side.

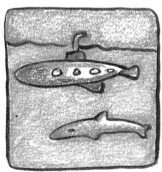

Submarines are designed to copy a fish's cylindrical body. They are tapered at the ends, and broad sides mimic the pectoral fins of fishes.

Photo, facing page, courtesy Steinhart Aquarium/Photo Researchers, Inc.

What Big Teeth You Have!

Atlantic Wolf Fish (*Anarhichas lupas*)

Scaleless and snakelike in body shape, the Atlantic wolf fish may grow to a length of 5 feet and weigh as much as 30 pounds. Its reddish-brown body is striped with black and adorned with a long dorsal fin. It swims in the waters of the Atlantic Ocean off the American coasts as well as European coasts and the North Sea.

Atlantic wolf fishes use their great, toothy jaws to crush and crunch crustaceans and mollusks (including hard-shelled mussels, sea urchins, and starfishes). Shells and all are swallowed.

All nine species of wolf fishes (including wolf eels) are aggressive. Some species are fished commercially in North American and European waters where they are called catfishes. They have been known to bite through wood planks and hard leather boots after they've been caught.

Astronauts underwater! Fishes and water are almost the same density, so fishes are living in a weightless world. Unlike humans, fishes don't need their skeletons to support their body weight, so their bones are often extra-light.

400-million-year-old-fishes! The coelacanth (SEAL-ah-kanth) is alive and swimming today, although scientists used to believe the species had become extinct 80 million years ago. In 1938, science rediscovered them in South Africa when a fisherman fished one from the sea. It seems local people hadn't realized they were catching fossils.

Photo, facing page, courtesy Tom McHugh/Photo Researchers, Inc.

FISHES

Pacific Lamprey (*Lampetra tridentata*)

Like their relatives, the hagfishes, lampreys are jawless, eellike, and weirder than weird looking. But unlike marine hagfishes, lampreys spend their lives in fresh water, or, if they are marine species, they return to fresh water to spawn their eggs. And while hagfishes prey on dead or dying fish, some lampreys prey on the living.

Many lampreys are parasites; they attach themselves by mouth and teeth to a fish's skin and suck out blood and body fluids. The mouth glands of lampreys secrete anticoagulants—substances that keep the blood of their prey flowing. When they have sucked out all of a host's juices, they look for fresh prey.

Lampreys also use their mouths, or suckers, to anchor themselves to rocks, to carry stones to their nest, or for mating. During egg fertilization, the female attaches herself to a stone while the male attaches himself to the female—both using their suckers. Lamprey eggs hatch into burrowing larvae, and they remain in that life stage for 3 to 6 years before they mature. The change from larvae to adult may take 8 months, and during this time, lampreys cannot and do not feed. When the change is complete, parasitic lampreys begin to feed on the fluids of other fishes while nonparasitic lampreys simply breed and die.

There are about 24 species of lampreys found in temperate climates all over the world. Fourteen species live in the waters of North America, including the Great Lakes. The Pacific lamprey grows to a length of 27 inches. It is a marine species that thrives in the Pacific Ocean.

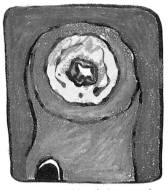

Earth's first fishes appeared about 500 million years ago. Although they had backbones, they were jawless, finless, and scaleless—unlike most of their modern descendants. How do we know? Fish skeletons make good fossils because they were once made of bone.

Lampreys and hagfishes are the only jawless fishes living today. They feed solely by sucking or scraping their prey.

Visit a museum or a fossil store in your neighborhood. See if you are able to spot individual scales, fins, spines, and even eyes—all fossilized. Remember, these fishes were in the swim millions of years ago!

Photo, facing page, courtesy Rondi/Tandi/Photo Researchers, Inc.

FISHES

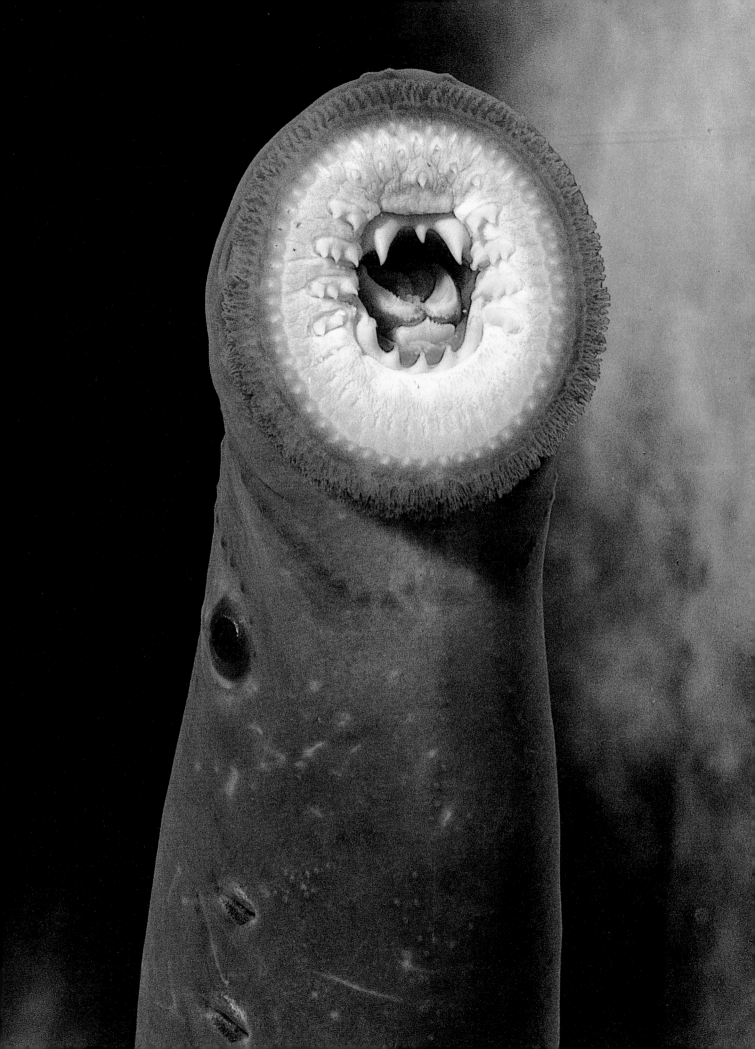

Dragons of the Deep

Leafy Seadragon (*Phyllopteryx eques*)

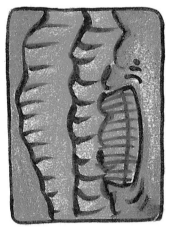

Is it a vine? A weed? An exotic plant from outer space? Actually, it is an extremely leafy seadragon camouflaged to look like the seaweed, algae, and eel grass common in the Australian coastal waters where it lives.

Like its relative, the sea horse, the male leafy seadragon is the one who cares for the eggs. He doesn't have a pouch (like the male sea horse). Instead, he packs the eggs below his tail where the skin becomes especially spongy. This happens before the male and female seadragons mate. After the female deposits her eggs underneath the male's tail, his skin hardens into a separate pouch for each egg. When the baby seadragons are ready to swim on their own, out they pop!

Like sea horses, leafy seadragons are not swift swimmers. Instead of speed, they depend on camouflage to avoid predators. Seadragons can change their reddish-brown color to match sea plants, and their leafy limbs sway in the ocean like weeds.

From the horse's mouth! Ancient legend has it that sea horse and seadragon remains could cure leprosy, infertility, and rabies, but that's just a tall tale.

In many species of fishes, males are in charge of "child care." Male sea catfish carry eggs and fry by mouth, and male pipefish brood eggs.

A sea horse uses the feathery fin on its back to travel. This fin vibrates as many as 70 times each second, and each vibration is a complete wave action that ripples top to bottom through the fin. A pair of pectoral fins behind the sea horse's head provides turning and steering power.

Photo, facing page, courtesy Paul A. Zahl/Photo Researchers, Inc.

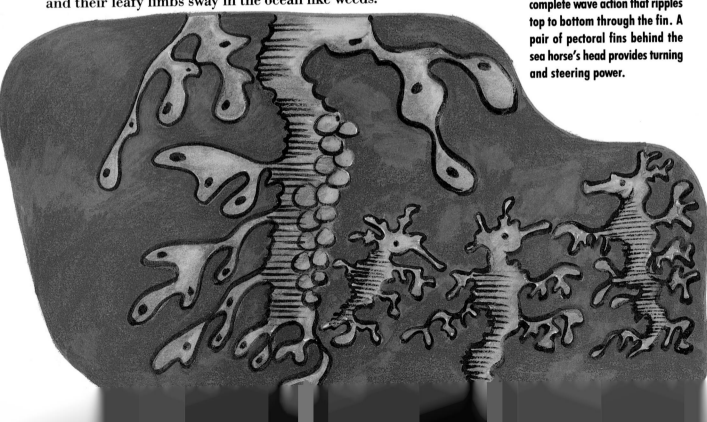

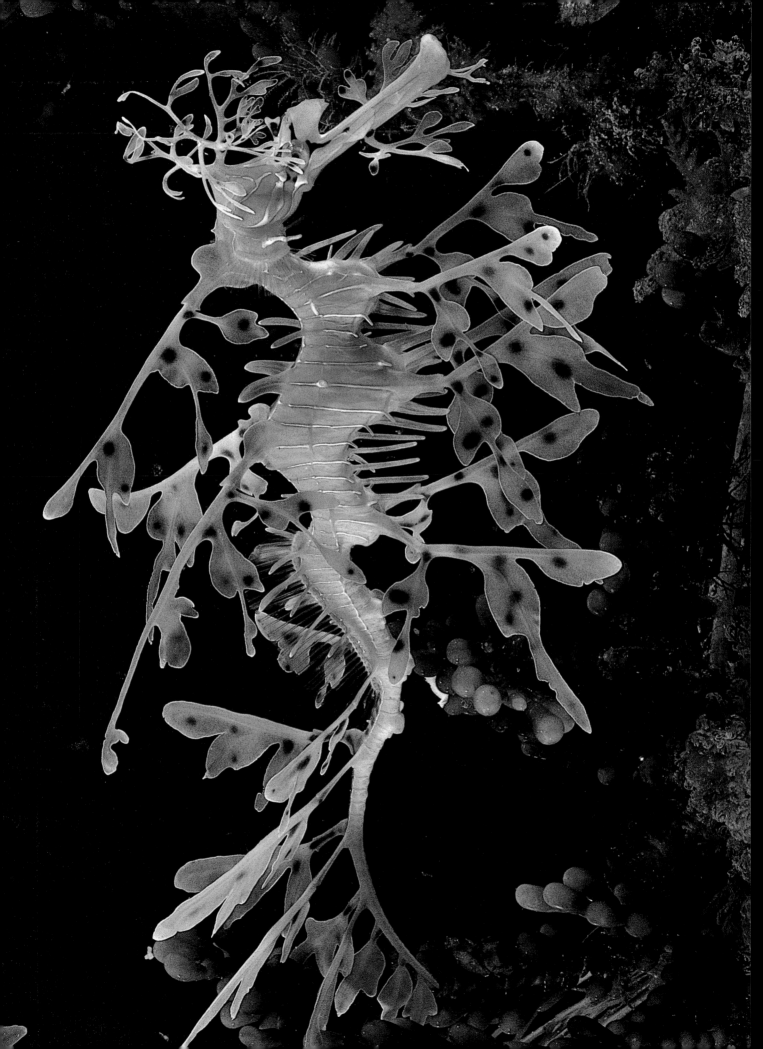

The Better to Eat Who With?

SOUTH AMERICAN HORNED FROG (*Ceratophrys ornata*)

The South American horned frog has a powerful jaw and sharp, toothlike fangs— the better to eat small mammals, snakes, birds, turtles, and other frogs. This frog likes to sit and wait for prey to pass by. Its colorful, armored skin provides great camouflage among leaves, dirt, and grasses where it burrows so deeply that only its bulging eyes are visible.

Most relatives of the South American horned frog are odd-looking. Many have body armor—thick shields of dense skin covering their back and head—that makes them too much of a mouthful for predators to swallow. Some species grow to eight inches long and almost as wide; others are tiny, barely one inch long when fully grown.

When the rainy season ends, the South American horned frog is one of a group of species that burrow into the ground and form cocoons to encase their bodies. The cocoon is like parchment and is made of layers of dried skin and mucous secretions. It encases the entire frog except for two air vents at the nostrils. Once in their cocoons, frogs can live for many months (maybe even years), and then . . . just add water!

Waterproof! Frogs are amphibians, which means they are "creatures that live in both places"—in water and on land. Frogs need water to mate, lay eggs, raise tadpoles, and just to survive. In order to conserve water, frogs have developed surprising ways to "waterproof" themselves in dry seasons. Waterproofing keeps the water in, not out. Some frogs form cocoons and stay encased for months; others ooze a waxy mucous that shields them during the day when they're not very active.

FROGS

RED-EYED TREE FROG *(Agalychnis callidryas)*

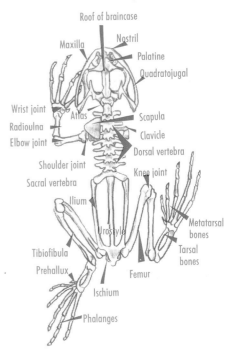

What's neon green and has blue racing stripes, orange toes, a creamy belly, and blood-red eyes with an elliptical or catlike pupil? The red-eyed tree frog, of course. This little tree frog hangs out at night (which means it is nocturnal) in the tropical forests of Central America. With long, sticky toe pads resembling small suction discs and opposable first and second fingers and toes (they can touch each other), the red-eyed tree frog can grasp twigs and branches like a high-flying monkey. This acrobatic ability comes in handy to avoid predators, devour insects, and even to impress a potential mate.

A male in search of a female will call from his perch on the branches hanging high—sometimes fifty feet high!—above a quiet stretch of water. A responsive female will join him, lay a clutch of fifty-or-so eggs on a leaf, and protect them with a thick layer of jelly. When tiny tadpoles hatch, they squirm their way out of the jelly and drop into the water far below. There, they grow for several months before the change into froglets is complete.

Frogs and toads are anurans, a type of "tailless" amphibian. Anurans have a basic anatomy that varies only slightly from species to species.

Frogs aren't the only animals that metamorphose, or change, into a different form during their lifetime. Butterflies metamorphose from caterpillar to chrysalis to butterfly. There's even metamorphic rock—rock that under pressure, heat, or chemical action, has changed its original structure.

FROGS

TORQUOISE POISON DART FROG (*Dendrobates auratus*)

Deep in the tropical forests of Central and South America, torquoise poison dart frogs and their relatives boast brightly colored skin that is also very poisonous. These frogs (like most amphibians) have two types of skin glands: one produces slimy mucous to keep in moisture and to act as a sealant; the other produces poison to discourage predators from dining on frog's legs. The frog's bright colors may serve as a warning to hungry enemies: "Don't eat me, I'm toxic!"

Frogs are immune to their own poison, although the scientists who study them aren't sure why. And some predators—especially certain snakes—can eat these frogs without harm. But most small animals will get sick, even die, if they devour a poison frog.

While poisonous skin is very important to these frogs because it protects them from enemies, it has long been valued by the people who live in the tropical forests for a different reason. Small monkeys and birds shot by darts dipped in the dart frog's poison are instantly paralyzed. When animals are hunted this way, they are not poisonous for people to eat. Over the centuries, people in the rain forests have learned to use the natural resources around them to survive and to live in harmony with nature.

Hunters in the rain forest use very little poison for their darts. To collect it, they must find a poison dart frog, kill it, and roast it over a fire. The heat causes the glands in the frog's skin to sweat tiny drops of poison. The poison is scraped off the skin and saved in a container until it ferments. Darts dipped in the mixture are dried before hunting.

FROGS

A Swell Toad

THE SURINAM TOAD (Pipa pipa)

The South American Surinam toad could easily be mistaken for a flat, square mud pie with two beady eyes. This blackish-brown creature sometimes grows to a length of eight inches and is perfectly camouflaged for the muddy waters of the Amazon and Orinoco rivers where it lives and reproduces.

Surinam toads have a unique way of raising their young. As the female deposits her eggs in water, her mate has a special job to do—he must carefully maneuver 60 to 80 eggs onto the female's back where she will carry them until they hatch.

After the male has completed his task, he retreats, and the female sits quietly for several hours. While she waits, the skin on her back swells up like a sponge and surrounds each egg in a tiny capsule of tissue. Within four months' time, fully formed young toadlets emerge from their mother's back.

All frogs have very sensitive skin, and some even breathe through it. (Of course, frogs also use their lungs to breathe.) Because frogs and other amphibians have such sensitive skin, they are good indicators of environmental conditions. Problems like acid rain, contaminated air and water, and exposure to high levels of ultraviolet sun rays affect frog populations. In fact, concerned scientists are studying a worldwide decline in amphibians.

ing page, courtesy Animals Animals © OSF, Avril Ramage

GRASS FROG *(Ptychadena anchietae)*

Frogs are "loudmouths" when it comes to defending territory, attracting mates, or sending out an SOS. Frogs of both sexes will make a very loud noise when in distress. Distress calls are usually sharp or shrill sounds that have been known to catch potential predators off-guard, allowing the frogs making all that noise to escape.

Male frogs, using their balloon-like vocal sacs, can advertise their intentions. Scientists recognize three types of advertisement calls: courtship—to attract a mate; territorial—to warn off neighboring males; encounter—when two aggressive males are too close for comfort.

Males of some frog species have a single vocal sac; male South African grass frogs have two. When a male grass frog calls, both sacs fill with air, and they look like double bubbles.

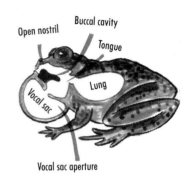

VOCAL SAC DIAGRAM

The International Union for Conservation of Nature has formed a special amphibian group as part of the Species Survival Commission to actively encourage amphibian conservation. If you want to learn how you can help, write: IUCN Species Survival Commission, C/O Chicago Zoological Society, Brookfield, IL 60503.

FROGS

Photo, facing page, courtesy Animals Animals © Michael Fogden

WATER-HOLDING FROG *(Cyclorana cultripes)*

When the rains begin to fall on the rough terrain of the Australian Outback, water-holding frogs don't waste one drop. They burrow out from their underground caves, hurry to the nearest puddle or pool of water, and gorge on swarms of insects freshly hatched. Still in a hurry, water-holding frogs mate, spawn, and their tadpoles metamorphose into young adults.

When the rainy season draws to an end, and the water begins to dry up, they absorb as much water as possible into special sacs beneath their skin. As the sacs swell, the frogs look as if they are surrounded by floppy water balloons. Water-holding frogs then burrow back down to their caves, and their bodies become covered with a cocoon that looks like dry cellophane and is made of their own mucous and skin cells. This cocoon holds in the water they absorbed aboveground. So water-holding frogs can survive for two or three years, maybe more, until the next rainfall.

A frog's tongue is sticky and attached to the front of its mouth. Most frogs have teeth too tiny for chewing, and food is swallowed whole. When it swallows, a frog's eyes sink back in its head and push food down its throat.

Are those raindrops or white walls? Another desert amphibian, the North American desert spadefoot toad, comes out of its burrow when it feels the vibrations of desert rains. Unfortunately, off-road vehicles make the ground "sound" just like rain to the toads; if they come up when it's dry, they die.

Adult amphibians don't drink water. Instead, they absorb it through their skin.

F R O G S

PANAMANIAN GOLDEN FROG (*Atelopus zeteki*)

Bright yellow means slow down for trouble—the Panamanian golden frog is poisonous (toxic). Like most species of frogs with skin toxins, the golden frog is brightly colored. These are called warning colors. Herpetologists believe that predators learn to avoid frogs with warning colors.

Not only are these frogs toxic, they're also noxious, which means they taste bad. After one yucky mouthful, a predator is warned that bad taste goes with bright colors. That's called "learned behavior."

Some frogs are copy-frogs. They look poisonous because of their bright colors, but they're actually harmless mimics. The *Eleutherodactylus gaigeae*, a nontoxic frog, looks almost identical to another, highly toxic frog, *Phyllobates lugubris*. Both frogs have the same skin color and pattern and they live in the same areas, but only one is poisonous. If you were a hungry predator, would you take a chance on a toxic mouthful?

Phyllobates terribilis is one of the largest species of toxic frogs. One *terribilis* contains enough poison to kill about 20,000 white mice.

FROGS

RED AND GREEN DART POISON FROG *(Dendrobates granuliferus)*

Dart poison frogs and their relatives in the Central and South American rain forests come in a rainbow of colors—hot scarlet, neon yellow, and electric blue. They can also be identified by a pair of muscular pads on the upper side of their fingertips and toes.

After the eggs of dart poison frogs hatch, the tadpoles crawl onto one parent's back; whether they choose the male or female parent depends on their species. Who totes the tadpoles?

With red and green dart poison frogs, it's the female, but with torquoise poison dart frogs, it's the male. The tadpoles are then carried to water, where they swim away and must learn to fend for themselves.

Some dart poison frogs are terrestrial, which means they spend most of their time on the ground. Others are arboreal— they live in trees. But all arrow poison frogs need to be near water so their young can develop from eggs to small adult frogs.

Naturalists study the world and its many creatures. Over the centuries, naturalists have developed a system to classify living creatures—how they're different and how they're the same. This way of grouping and classifying is called "taxonomy," and it gives scientists a universal system to keep track of evolution as living things change and develop over time.

The red and green poison dart frog, *Dendrobates granuliferus*, is from the Kingdom: Animalia; Phylum: Chordata; Class: Amphibia; Order: Anura; Family: Dendrobatidae; Genus: *Dendrobates*; Species: *granuliferus*.

FROGS

HARLEQUIN FROG (Atelopus varius)

At first glance, you might think the harlequin frog from the mountains of South America is wearing a bright green and black clown suit. This frog is poisonous as well as colorful. Even the eggs of the harlequin frog contain poisons that attack the nervous system; this helps discourage predators like snakes, birds, fish, and small mammals from lunching on froggy caviar.

The harlequin frog's tadpoles develop in fast-running streams. Like all creatures, they have adapted to their environment in special ways. Harlequin tadpoles have very big mouths and many rows of tiny teeth. Big mouths mean they can eat a lot; it also means they can hang on. Fast-running streams have very strong currents, and the tadpole's mouth acts as a suction disc to attach it to rocks. Without these "suction cups," the tadpoles would wash away downstream. The suction works so well, herpetologists must pry the tadpoles from the rocks in order to study them.

A "lingual flip" isn't dessert. It is the way most frogs guarantee themselves a tasty meal. A) The tongue flips up inside the mouth. B) Bull's-eye! C) The tongue returns to the frog's mouth and resumes its flip.

146

FROGS

PYGMY MARSUPIAL FROG *(Flectonotus pygmaeus)*

The female pygmy marsupial frog from South America carries her eggs in a natural backpack called a dorsal pouch. This tiny frog can tote as many as nine eggs that will take about twenty-five days to develop into tadpoles. Once the eggs are in the pouch, the female carries her precious cargo alone, but she needs help packing her pouch in the first place.

That's the job of the male pygmy marsupial frog. When pygmy marsupial frogs are ready to mate, the male places his toes inside the opening of the female's pouch. As she drops each egg, the male rotates it with his heels and pops it into the female's pouch with his pelvis. Scientists believe each egg is fertilized as it rotates.

Tree frogs have "sticky fingers" or toe pads that grip branches, leaves, and even glass. They can climb the wall with ease.

Ancient Egyptians worshiped the goddess Heket who had the head of a frog. She was a symbol for life-giving change when grain turned into seed and could be planted for food. In India and South America, frogs are worshiped for bringing rain. Asian myths credit the frog with holding the world on its back. Fairy tale frogs, like "the Frog King," often represent our human ability to grow, mature, and become better beings.

FROGS

ASIATIC GLIDING FROG *(Rhacophorus nigropatmus)*

It's a bird. It's a plane. It's the Asiatic gliding frog! This amazing frog makes its home high above the jungle floor in tree branches. Because the Asiatic gliding frog has long toes and fingers that are webbed, it can glide for distances of forty or fifty feet. As it cruises through the air, the gliding frog spreads its fingers and toes and holds them stiff. At the same time, the frog scoops up its belly to enhance its aerodynamic abilities. Although real flight demands a whole different anatomy, gliding frogs do have some control over the length and direction of each glide. A "flight" begins from a high tree trunk, heads downward at a diagonal, and ends at the base of a distant tree. The Asiatic gliding frog and its relatives have catlike pupils that dilate in dim light so they can spot tiny insects in the deep, dark forests where they live.

Rhacophorus reinwardtii, a relative of the gliding frog, is known as the "flying frog" because it, too, can glide through the air with the greatest of ease.

Some frogs can leap 40 times their length. What makes these "leap frogs" go? Super strong muscles in their hind legs and sticky hind feet provide oomph and traction.

Arf, arf! The barking tree frog sounds just like. . .you guessed it.

FROGS

TURTLE FROG *(Myobatrachus gouldii)*

How do frogs know that dinner is ready? Do they see it, hear it, or smell it? That depends on the frog. Woodhouse toads are attracted to insects by the sounds they make, and some cannibalistic frogs listen for the sound of dinner calling, croaking, or ribeting; the South American horned frog and other "sit-and-wait" strategists like to see their prey. Scientists believe turtle frogs are attracted by smell to the termites they love to eat.

When turtle frogs are ready to mate in the deserts of Western Australia, females approach calling males above the ground. Together, they burrow underground (sometimes as far as 1 meter, about 3 feet) and remain for five or six months before the female finally deposits her eggs. The eggs are tended underground, and when they hatch, fully formed froglets appear.

Scientists believe that ancient relatives of the turtle frog were present in Australia, Antarctica, and parts of Asia as long as 140 million years ago.

Bizarre broods! The gastric brooding frog is a relative of the turtle frog. Female gastric brooders carry their eggs in their stomach. There, the tadpoles develop. When they are ready to hatch, the female opens her *mouth*, and froglets hop out. Because of this unusual brooding ability, scientists have tried to study this frog. Sadly, the gastric brooder is endangered, perhaps extinct.

F R O G S

TOMATO FROG *(Dyscophus antongilii)*

The tomato frog from Madagascar is named after its shiny red skin. Herpetologists believe there are very few species related to the tomato frog. Even though little is known about them, many exotic frog species are collected for sale in pet stores around the world. Although these frogs can be raised in terrariums, they are never able to return to their native habitat. There is a wonderful way to study amphibian metamorphosis and help conserve frog populations in your neighborhood. If you live near a pond or stream, you may discover frog or toad spawn (eggs) in the spring. Frog spawn looks like a cloudy lump. Toad spawn is deposited in long strings. Gently collect a very small amount of spawn and some water weeds and keep these in an aquarium (not in direct sunlight) with several inches of water.

Change and dechlorinate the water every two or three days. Fish pellets can provide nourishment for the tadpoles. When arms and legs develop and tails begin to shrink, the tadpoles will need both water and land. There are simple ways to create a healthy frog habitat inside a terrarium. Ask an expert at your neighborhood pet store or school for ideas. Adult amphibians eat moving insects like baby crickets, flies, and beetles. While the weather is still warm, frogs and toads should be returned to the spawning pond and released.

What's the difference between a toad and a frog? Probably nothing! Commonly, what is known as a frog in one part of the world might be called a toad in another. Herpetologists have given up using either name to classify amphibians. Instead, they use scientific names.

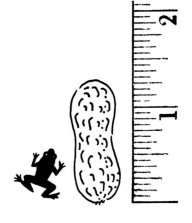

The little grass frog is the smallest North American frog. It's about the size of a peanut.

FROGS

GLASS FROG (Centrolenella orientalis)

In the forests of Latin America, the male glass frog has the job of "guard frog" looking after the eggs he has fertilized. When the female glass frog is ready to mate, she is attracted to the calling male, and she deposits her eggs on the underside of leaves and fronds where the male fertilizes them. The female is then free to go about her frog business, and the male is left behind to care for the eggs until they hatch into tadpoles. Often, a male will fertilize the eggs of more than one female. In that case, he must look after several broods. Glass frogs grow to a size of about 21 millimeters, which is a little smaller than a 25-cent piece. This particular glass frog is almost see-through and looks a bit like a lime jello mold.

Some insect larvae (or maggots) live as parasites on the eggs of frogs. Eggs that have parasites have an odd shape and will not survive to hatch into tadpoles. Some species of glass frogs with very strong "guarding behavior" will eat damaged eggs to destroy the parasites and save healthy eggs. Look closely at the eggs in this photo. Can you pick out the parasitized eggs in one corner?

FROGS

Photo, facing page, courtesy Animals Animals © OSF, G. I. Bernard

MASKED PUDDLE FROG (Smilisca phaeota)

The tiny green and yellow masked puddle frog likes to sleep in a furled leaf, hidden from hungry predators who also live in the rain forests of South America. Puddle frogs lay eggs in filmy clutches on top of warm, still waters. These frogs and their relatives are known to produce as many as six egg clutches in a single breeding season. That means lots and lots of masked puddle frogs are hatched each year.

The ability to produce future generations is very important to the survival of every species. Frogs who live in the humid tropics (like the masked puddle frog) have continuous reproduction. That means they may deposit many different egg clutches each year. Frogs that live in drier climates with seasonal rainfall may produce only one egg clutch per year. Hatch rates for particular frogs vary from one or two froglets to as many as 80,000 in one year!

Leaping frogs wear goggles. Not the kind you buy at the store but special see-through eyelids that cover and protect frog eyes from water and dirt. When a frog jumps, these eyelids close.

The Celebrated Jumping Frog of Calaveras County, by Mark Twain, tells the story of a red-legged frog and a frog-jumping contest. Years after the story was published, people in Calaveras County, California, decided a real frog-jumping contest would be a good idea. Each year, kids and adults train frogs for this famous event. Because the red-legged frog is endangered, other frogs win by a nose.

F R O G S

BRUSH-SNOUTED WEEVIL (*Rhina barbirostris*)

Weevils are beetles with very long heads, and their eyes, elbowed antennae, and mouthparts are set far apart from each other. The family known as true weevils (numbering at least 50,000 species) is the largest in the entire animal kingdom. True weevils are sometimes called snout beetles, elephant beetles, and billbugs because most sport an extremely long proboscis, or snout.

True weevils are herbivores (they feed only on plants), and they live all over the world. They have a reputation as pests because they often bore into wood, leaves, seeds, and other plant tissue.

The brush-snouted weevil is a large beetle from South America and Trinidad. It is also called the palm weevil because its larvae burrow into the trunks of coconut palms, killing the trees. Like many other animals, true weevils are most numerous in warmer regions of the world.

Biting jaws at the very tip of the weevil's snout (rostrum) are used to chomp down, while the snout itself is a drilling tool. The snout-weevil's antennae elbow out from either side of the snout. At each antenna's tip, a "hairy" club allows the weevil to sense the plant seed or stem surface into which it is drilling.

The largest true weevils reach a length of three inches, but on the average, they are less than one-fourth of an inch.

Photo, facing page, courtesy Animals Animals © Michael Fogden

INSECTS

PEANUT-HEAD BUG (*Fulgora servillei*)

The bulbous peanut-head bug has an eye-catching way to frighten hungry predators. It depends on an extra set of very large eyespots located on its hind wings. When the peanut-head bug opens its wings and flashes its giant "eyes," it buys time to escape from a predator who might mistake the "eyes" for those of its own enemies.

The peanut-head bug is a member of the fulgorid group, or the "lantern flies." *Fulgor* is Latin for "flash of lightning," but the name is based on folklore. People used to believe that the large head of a fulgorid would glow in the dark like a lantern; now scientists have proved it to be a no glow.

Even though they don't shine in the dark, there is no denying fulgorids are extremely weird. They often sport nifty colors, and they always have huge heads! They live in Mexico, Central America, and other tropical regions where they feed on plant juices.

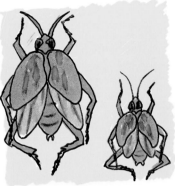

True bugs belong to the order Hemiptera (he-MIP-te-rah); that is, their hind wings are thin and clear, and their front wings are thick at the base but thin at the tip. True bugs have a life cycle that includes incomplete metamorphosis; the young nymphs look and act much like the adult bug.

Instead of two pairs of wings, flies have one wing pair and nubby balancing organs (halteres). These help the fly control roll, pitch, and yaw and land upside down. They act a bit like a fly gyroscope.

Photo, facing page, courtesy Animals Animals © Doug Wechsler

INSECTS

HARLEQUIN BUG (*Tectocoris diophthalmus*)

Most insects hatch from eggs; while some emerge as larvae (caterpillars, maggots, or grubs), others look almost like adults of their species. If they also grow up without going through a pupal (resting) stage, their life cycle involves *incomplete* metamorphosis. Harlequin bugs change markings slightly as they pass from egg to young nymph (see facing page) and later nymph stages, but basically, they look much the same as when they hatched.

The most advanced insects have a life cycle that includes *complete* metamorphosis. Metamorphosis means change of body form, and stages of complete metamorphosis—egg, larvae, and adult—all are distinct from each other.

In complete metamorphosis, a larva emerges from its egg with simple eyes and a soft body that hardens quickly. A larva will often devour its egg shell, consuming important minerals, before it searches for other food. After it has grown and molted (shed) its cuticle, or skin, the larva will attach itself to a leaf and begin to pupate. For the final time, the larval cuticle is shed, and the exposed pupal cuticle hardens immediately.

During the pupal stage, the insect's entire body is re-formed. Nerves and muscles dissolve, and new ones are created. When this process is complete, the young adult insect slowly emerges from a split in the pupal skin.

It may take several hours before the newly free adult insect is able to travel. During this time, it is very vulnerable to predators. Surviving insects may not develop their full color markings for more than a week.

This harlequin bug is a nymph. In Greek and Roman mythology, a nymph is a nature goddess. In entomology (the study of insects), a nymph is the young of any insect whose life cycle does not include complete metamorphosis. It is also another name for a pupa, which is an insect in the stage of development between larva and adult.

Most insects have a life cycle of only one year, but some may live for two or more (especially in temperate climates). They may spend the winter as a nymph or pupa, becoming an adult the following spring or summer.

INSECTS

SHIELD STINKBUG (*Lyramorpha* sp.)

Stinkbugs are just that—stinky. They discharge a smelly liquid from two pores on their underside when they're disturbed. This is a good way of keeping hungry predators—who don't want a stinky mouthful—at bay.

Stinkbugs can be recognized by their very broad, convex bodies that are often brown or metallic. Some species are more colorful and sport shades of red, orange, black, or blue in assorted patterns.

Stinkbugs are also known as shield bugs because they have a scutellum, or shield, that covers the hind part of their body. Sometimes the female uses it to shield her eggs and young when she sits over them. The stinkbugs pictured here are nymphs, which means they are not yet fully mature. They look much like adult stinkbugs of their genus. These stinkbugs live in Australia.

A few of the 5,000 or so known species of stinkbugs prey on other insects, but most feed on fruit juices. People often consider stinkbugs pests because they damage fruits, vegetables, and other plants as they feed. The problem is greatest when a species overpopulates, but as farmers and gardeners learn more about insects, they are finding ways to control pest populations without the use of poisonous pesticides.

Bombardier beetles blast curious predators with a noisy jet of boiling chemicals fired from the rear. Some species spray in speedy spurts—500 per second! Two chemicals—stored in the beetle's abdomen—mix when fired, and the result repels predators such as spiders, birds, frogs, mice, and ants.

One Asian stinkbug can squirt its smelly secretions for a distance of 12 inches, and it makes a loud noise at the same time!

INSECTS

Here's Looking at You

HORSEFLY (*Chrysops* sp.)

Although horseflies look as if they are wearing great sunglasses, those shades are actually eyes—compound eyes, that is. Most insects have compound eyes that are made up of hundreds of simple eyes placed together. Each simple eye—really designed to detect motion and light—"sees" only a part of the picture. It's up to the insect's brain to piece together the pictures like a jigsaw puzzle.

Typically, insects have two very large compound eyes located toward the front and sides of their head and three simple eyes (called ocelli) on top. What would you see if you looked through an insect's eyes? Scientists know that a bee on a flower can see an animal move several yards away. But does the bee know whether the animal is a horse or a dog, or is it just a moving shape? Lots of insects see colors. (Bees and butterflies see a broader spectrum than we do!) But are beetles color-blind? Probably. If you study insects and their senses, you might be able to answer these questions some day.

All 2,500 species of horseflies have compound eyes. In males, these eyes take up most of the surface of the head. *Chrysops*, and many other species, boast an especially beautiful rainbow of iridescent hues that band or spot the eyes.

Horseflies can be as small as a house fly or as long as more than an inch. Female horseflies are pesky critters because they feed on the blood of other animals, including humans. They cut through a victim's skin using their short, sharp mouthparts, and then they lap up flowing blood. Horseflies rarely transmit diseases that affect humans, but they do carry some animal diseases.

How touching. Insects depend on thousands of sensory hairs fringing the surface of their body to tell them what's what. These hairs are connected to nerve endings. When an insect moves its leg, it also moves its leg hairs. Then, the insect's brain receives the message that its leg is bent.

Some horseflies (such as *Chrysops*) are also known as deer flies and moose flies because they prey on you know who. Because common names vary so much from place to place, scientists give each plant and animal a scientific name that is used the world over.

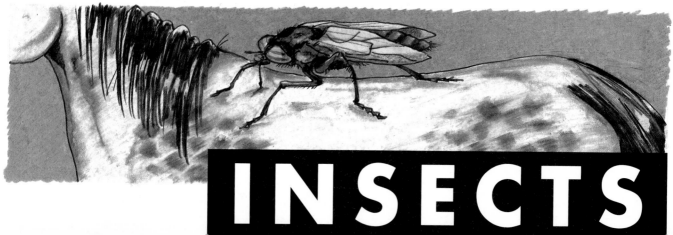

INSECTS

NET-WINGED BEETLE (*Lycus* sp.)

The net-winged beetle flies very slowly and clumsily, so it can't depend on a quick getaway to avoid predators. Instead, its body fluids are so bad-tasting and bitter that predators, warned by its bright colors and patterns, sometimes stay away.

Net-winged beetles have soft bodies and leathery-looking front wings. Usually, each wing is wide at the tip and narrow at the base. Often, their head lengthens into a beak, and their bodies have bright yellow and black bands, stripes, or spots that make them hard to miss as they cling to plants and flowers.

There are about 3,000 species of net-winged beetles. They live mostly in tropical areas. They hunt for snails and insects and, in turn, are hunted by birds and monkeys.

Beetles, frogs, fishes, and many other animals depend on brightly colored bodies to warn predators to stay away! Predators learn quickly to connect bright warning colors with a very yucky taste.

Copy moths! Some species of moths have evolved into almost perfect mimics of net-winged beetles. Since they sport the same bright warning colors and patterns of the bad-tasting beetles, predators avoid them.

What's so special about a beetle? For one thing, a beetle boasts a pair of tough front wings (elytra) that protect the delicate hind wings folded underneath. A beetle's skeleton is sturdier than that of many insects; and its primitive mouthparts are able to chew solid food.

Photo, facing page, courtesy Animals Animals © Michael Fogden

INSECTS

GULF FRITILLARY BUTTERFLY (*Agraulis vanillae*)

The gulf fritillary (also known as the silver-spotted flambeau) lives in Central and South America. The adult is famous for the beautiful silver patches on the underside of its hind wing.

In its larval stage—as a caterpillar—the gulf fritillary feeds on the leaves of passion flowers. It is protected from some predators, such as birds, by its extremely stiff and sticky barbed spines. Unfortunately, even the stickiest spines are no protection against predatory wasps. After one sting, the wasp deposits its egg in the paralyzed body of the caterpillar. When the wasp larva hatches, it feeds on the flesh of its host.

Adult fritillaries (and all other butterflies) feed on liquid nectar that they suck in through their extremely long proboscis, or tube-shaped feeding organ. When it's not at work, the butterfly's proboscis curls up for handy storage.

A butterfly's body is covered with tiny scales that seem to "know" which way the wings fold after flight.

Butterflies probably acquired their name when common yellow butterflies reminded someone of flying butter.

Insects rely on keen taste organs located around their jaw. Some insects "feel" taste using their antennae. Some butterflies have taste organs on their feet; these are so sensitive, the butterfly's proboscis automatically uncoils at the first touch of a tasty flower.

INSECTS

Spooky Sphinx

DEATH'S-HEAD SPHINX (*Acherontia atropos*)

Like all members of its family, the death's-head sphinx moth is such a powerful flyer, its beating wings seem to disappear in a blur. But when it comes to travel and feeding, this moth is the exception, not the rule.

Most sphinx moths fly from flower to flower feeding on nectar with their extremely long proboscis, but the death's-head sphinx uses its short tongue to pierce honeycomb in beehives and suck honey. Sphinx moths hardly ever travel long distances, but the death's-head sphinx regularly migrates from Africa to northern Europe.

It is easy to mistake sphinx moths for hummingbirds because they have a large body and a habit of hovering in front of a flower while they feed.

This moth earned its named because of the pattern on its thorax that resembles a human skull, but sphinx moths as a group are named for a habit they have as caterpillars. While resting, the caterpillars assume a peculiar position—head curved down below their thorax and the front part of their body raised—which is much like the posture of the Egyptian sphinx. The entire caterpillar looks like the front end of a very large—and very frightening—animal. This defensive, or threat, posture is an effective way to scare away hungry predators.

A tropical sphinx moth, *Erinnyis ello*, regularly commutes all the way from South America to Canada.

Handy wipes! Some butterflies use their two front legs to clean their eyes. They let their other four legs do the walking.

INSECTS

Photo, facing page, courtesy Animals Animals © Alistair Shay/OSF

Fiddling Forewings

FLAT-FACED KATYDID (*Lirometopum coronatum*)

Male katydids make music by winging it. One forewing is equipped with a file that is rubbed against a scraper on the other forewing. The sound is made louder when the katydid raises its forewings slightly to create a small resonant cavity, or "mini speaker."

Katydids, grasshoppers, crickets, and mole-crickets belong to the scientific order Orthoptera, which means "straight wing." All males of this order "sing" to attract a mate; both males and females have excellent hearing. (In a few species, females are also capable of singing.) The katydid's tympana (eardrums) are located on its front legs, just about where you would find your kneecap.

Most members of the Orthoptera can fly, although jumping—powered by their long, strong hind legs—is their preferred method of locomotion. If you've ever tried to catch a katydid, you know what excellent jumpers they really are!

Some katydids have an extremely weird way of defending themselves from predators; it's called "reflex bleeding." Blood flows from the thorax or is squirted from the first joint of the leg. Certain species aim with great accuracy and always hit the bull's-eye.

Locusts are famous for swarming. On each major continent, there exist one or more species of locusts prone to population explosions. When this happens, millions of these locusts travel in mind-boggling swarms, and they may devour *all* vegetation in their path. Even the Bible mentions a plague of locusts.

Photo, facing page, courtesy Animals Animals © Michael Fogden

178

INSECTS

Leaf Me Alone

MALAYAN LEAF INSECT (*Phyllium pulchrifolium*)

Walkingsticks, like leaf insects, depend on camouflage for protection from predators; they mimic the sticks around them. Some walkingsticks can stay still for more than 6 hours at a time!

Huge Malayan leaf insects have wings and legs, and the sides of their body are flat and uneven like the edges of a leaf. To make matters even leafier, they are green, yellow, or brown.

During the day, they hang motionless, almost in a trance. When they do move, it is in slow motion, and they look like leaves blowing gently in the wind. Leaf insects have a special reflex action known as thanatosis, or playing dead. When they are startled, they automatically drop from their perch and stay perfectly still wherever they land.

Female leaf insects are flightless; they have lost their hind wings, although they do have leaflike front wings. Males *do* fly and are usually much smaller than females. The record length of a stick insect is 13 inches, but most are from 1 to 5 inches long.

All stick and leaf insects are herbivores (or plant eaters). Some species may reproduce in such numbers they can strip large areas of woodland. Commonly, they reproduce by parthenogenesis, which means the eggs are not fertilized by the male and develop into more females.

Malayan leaf insects of the genus Phyllium live in Malaysia and other areas of tropical Asia and Indonesia.

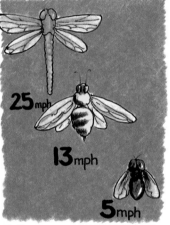

25mph

13mph

5mph

Call me speedy! Hawkmoths and dragonflies are the race cars of insects; they commonly cruise at 25 mph. Honeybees clock in at about 13 mph, butterflies at 12 mph, and house flies reach a slowpoke cruising speed of only 5 mph. And we still can't catch them!

INSECTS

Sticks and Stones

GIANT AUSTRALIAN STICK (*Extatosoma tiaratum*)

Walkingsticks and leaf insects all belong to the same scientific family: Phasmidae. As a group, they live mostly in the tropical areas of Asia, although some species have been seen as far north as Europe and North America. Members of this family come in a variety of shapes and colors, and they may resemble green, brown, or rotting leaves, thorns, grass, broken sticks, or stout twigs. One thing they all have in common is camouflage.

Many animals depend on a disguise—protective coloring or shape—to blend in with their background and to hide from predators. Camouflage is especially important for those animals that are not swift in the air or on the ground (a must for quick getaways) or who can't depend on other equipment—poison or armor, for instance—to keep danger away.

During the day, most stick and leaf insects stay almost completely motionless—in strange postures—made invisible by their resemblance to the plants and trees around them. Only the most alert bird or lizard can detect them in the stillness of daylight. They are most active under the cover of darkness, which is when they eat, mate, and drop their eggs.

Leaf insects have wings, but many species of stick insects do not. The giant Australian stick insect lives in Australia, of course.

Scent sense. Most insects have a sharp sense of smell. Some secrete smelly substances to ward off predators or attract mates.

Some of the Asian sticks qualify as the longest insects in the world. They reach a total length of more than one foot!

Photo, facing page, courtesy Animals Animals © R. H. Armstrong

INSECTS

DEWEY GREEN DARNER (*Anax junius*)

Darners are large, brightly colored dragonflies. Like all members of their family, they have a stout body, a large, movable head, and two pairs of large veiny wings. They also boast huge compound eyes (some can see in almost all directions at once, the better to spot their prey) and have biting and chewing mouthparts.

Dragonflies are fierce predators, and they pursue their prey—mosquitoes, flies, and gnats—on the wing. In flight, their bristly legs are used to clutch their victims while their long wings keep them airborne.

Dragonflies usually prefer habitats close to streams, lakes, and other permanent water sources. They need fresh water, in which their eggs hatch and the young reach maturity.

Dragonfly eggs are deposited in jellied masses that stick to water plants for several days. The newly hatched dragonfly nymph has no wings, and it may not mature for two or three years. During this immature stage of its life cycle, it lives completely underwater feeding on small fishes and tadpoles. When it grows large enough, the nymph crawls out of the water and molts to emerge as a fully winged dragonfly.

Darner species range from Alaska to Hawaii and the eastern coast of Asia. They are swift and graceful flyers whose wings are glassy; their abdomen is brilliant blue, and their brow is emerald green. Unlike most other dragonfies, adult darners can live far from water.

Skimmers are big colorful dragonflies often seen skimming shallow water or "sitting guard" on plants. They protect their territory from other dragonflies.

MMMMMM! Darners got their name because they were said to sew a child's mouth closed. But that's just a folktale!

To breathe underwater, the dewey green darner nymph uses internal gills that are in the form of ridges of tissue in its rectum. The nymph draws in and expels water across the ridges. If water is expelled very quickly, the nymph is jet propelled!

Photo, facing page, courtesy Animals Animals © John Gerlach

INSECTS

AMERICAN COCKROACH (*Periplaneta americana*)

Cockroaches; their primitive mouthparts are made for biting, and their long, slender legs are built for speed. The skittery sound of these pesky critters on the move is familiar to humans, because cockroaches have adapted to life most anywhere, especially in kitchens! Cockroaches are noisy on purpose; as they run, they drag the spurs at the ends of their legs on the ground to warn their fellows of danger. They may also produce smelly substances from their glands. Although they do have these warning signals, compared to many other insects, cockroaches are very primitive creatures.

Cockroaches are not very different from their fossilized ancestors. In fact, if you could travel back in time about 225 million years, you would probably see cockroaches (and other insects like dragonflies, leafhoppers, and cicadas) looking much as they do today. Cockroaches have stayed the same because they didn't *have* to change; they do an excellent job of surviving just as they are.

Like their ancestors, male cockroaches are winged. (In some species, both males and females sport wings.) The female cockroach produces two rows of eggs (a total of 30 or 40) inside a tough egg purse called an ootheca. She carries the purse on her abdomen until she finds a place to hide it. When the young are ready to hatch, they squeeze their way from the egg and through an opening in the purse.

The American cockroach lives in North America, but it originated in Africa. It grows to a length of about one inch (roughly 25 mm), which is small compared to its 3-inch-long tropical relatives.

Most insect fossils are of insect species who became extinct or evolved into different critters. Roaches and dragonflies are exceptions.

The first insect fossils date back about 345 million years and prove insects were living during the Carboniferous period. But entomologists know that insects have been around much longer than that because the fossils show many already distinctly different groups.

Fossils of the extremely large dragonfly *Meganeura monyi* show it had a wingspan of 3 feet!

Photo, facing page, courtesy Animals Animals © Bates Littlehales

INSECTS

CICADA (Family Cicadidae)

Cicadas, aphids, and treehoppers all belong to the scientific order Homoptera, and they are different from true bugs (order Hemiptera) because their beak is attached to the very back of the head, and their two pairs of wings are both transparent membranes. (Bugs, in contrast, have a leathery base on their front wings, which is why they are known as "half wings," or Hemiptera.)

Members of Homoptera reproduce in a variety of ways depending on the species. Some reproduce sexually, and some may produce eggs that develop without being fertilized. Those that don't lay eggs give birth to live young. Although their methods differ, all homopterans are extremely prolific when it comes to reproduction.

Some species of cicadas may swarm by the thousands, and there are more than 1,500 species in the world. Their wide head, huge compound eyes, and three, small simple eyes, or ocelli, in between make them easy to recognize.

Most female cicadas are mute, but males are famous for their "songs." These are made by two drumlike membranes inside their abdomen. A muscle causes each membrane to change shape, and this, in turn, produces vibration and sound. The noise is made louder by an amplifying cavity near the drums. The males use their tunes to attract females at mating time. Although males have ears, these don't work when cicadas are making music. (Maybe this protects the cicadas from their own noise!) In a few species, females can make as much music as males.

The periodical cicada is famous for its 17-year life cycle. Females lay their eggs in trees, and the nymphs hatch in six weeks and drop to the ground where they burrow. They remain in the earth for 17 years, crawl to the surface, and leave their old cuticles behind. Within weeks, the adult cicadas have found a mate, laid their eggs, and died. There are 13-year cicadas also.

After cicadas, grasshoppers and crickets are the noisest insects. They make their music by several methods: rubbing the rough edges at the base of both front wings together; drawing their hind leg over their forewing; rubbing their femur over their abdomen; striking a hind wing on a forewing; or by opening and closing their hind wings very quickly. The resulting vibrations produce lots of noise. To pick up these noisy signals, long-horned grasshoppers and crickets have ears on their front legs that act as aerials.

INSECTS

HORNED TREEHOPPER (*Umbonia crassicornis*)

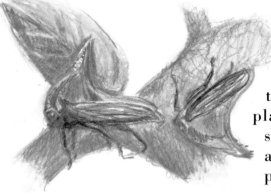

Treehoppers can be recognized by their unusual thorny or leaflike shape that is designed to match the thorny, leafy plants they live on. Their shape provides camouflage, allowing them to hide from potential predators.

Treehoppers and their close relatives, leafhoppers and spittlebugs, can best be recognized by their membranous wings that are raised rooflike over their body. They are all squatty and wedge-shaped, sporting short antennae and a small head, and they are known (and sometimes named) for their vigorous hopping ability.

Hoppers and spittlebugs are strict vegetarians who suck the juice from plants. To begin breaking down food before it reaches their stomach, they inject fluids into plants. These fluids are poisonous, and an infestation of treehoppers (or their kin) can cause stunted growth and discolored leaves on host plants.

Although they may be a gardener's foe, hoppers are fun to observe. Leafhoppers are often beautifully colored with bright yellow, red, green, and blue markings. Spittlebugs are less colorful and less energetic than hoppers when they are young. The horned treehopper lives in Florida and the New World tropics.

Female treehoppers often cut two parallel slices into the bark of a tree and deposit their eggs inside. In some species, the females tend the eggs carefully.

In 335 B.C., Aristotle compiled the *Historia animalium*, which described at least 300 animals. In Italy, more than 400 years later, Pliny the Elder used that work to research his own 37-volume *Historia naturalis*. In addition to real animals, Pliny included mermaids, unicorns, and winged horses in his natural history.

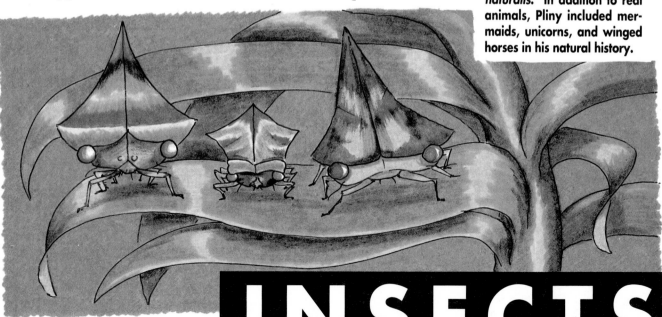

INSECTS

Gray Lesser Mouse Lemur *(Microcebus murinus)*

Primates! If some monkeys threw a primate party, the invitation list would include bush babies, sakis, monkeys, apes, chimpanzees, and you and me. What do we all have in common? Flexible hands with grasping fingers (usually with ten digits), relatively large brains, and a tree-dwelling lifestyle at some point in our evolution.

Of course, you would have some extremely weird dancing partners. Certain primates sport blue cheeks or red rear ends, while others wear punk hairdos. And they range in size from several ounces to more than 500 pounds. Watch out for your toes!

Mouse lemurs are pocket-sized critters, one of the world's smallest primates. They're also one of the oldest: their ancestors were among the very first primates on earth.

Mouse lemurs have a sweet tooth for fruit and honey, and insects are a favorite food. When eating beetles and grasshoppers, lemurs bite the soft belly of the bug first and make noisy smacking sounds. Lemurs are active during the day or night, depending on their species. To communicate with each other, lemurs chirrup, chatter, and even yodel from the tree of their choice.

Not all lemurs are tiny. In fact, they vary from rat to cat size. There are about 20 different types of lemurs, and they all live on Madagascar, a big island off the coast of Africa.

Ancient Romans believed the spirits of their dead roamed the night staring at the living with round glowing eyes and crying sadly. They called those ghosts "lemurs."

Sifakas are closely related to lemurs. Island natives believed these animals were sacred sun worshipers because they rise early to sunbathe in the trees.

The Prosimians may sound like a group of musicians or a football team, but they actually make up the largest group of primates. Prosimians look a lot like their primitive ancestors. Members of this group include lemurs, lorises, and tarsiers.

PRIMATES

Slow Loris (Nycticebus coucang)

This slowpoke prosimian would never be seen without its thick fur coat. Even at home in the tropics of Africa and Asia, the loris would die of cold without all of its fur. That's because a loris produces very little body heat energy. Low energy means a lazy routine and no fast footwork for these compact mammals. The slow loris dangles easily from branches and moves at a sloth's pace.

Lorises have bright big eyes that can see after dark, which is when they search for a variety of insects, birds, and eggs to eat. They have such short tails hidden under their fur, they are almost tailless. Thumbs and big toes point away from fingers and smaller toes, which means they are super opposable and able to grasp branches and twigs —just like your hands.

If you asked primates for a show of hands, they would all hold up their movable fingers. Some primates, chimpanzees, and humans, for example, can pick up a toothpick or a twig between their fingers and thumb. A loris uses its hand like a clamp to get a grip. Tree shrews have claws, and they use them to dig into branches. It might seem like a simple thing, but the ability to wrap fingers (and toes) around a branch is what made primates the masters of the trees. Because our ancestors developed this ability, they could climb higher without falling, reach more food, and grow bigger!

When a slow loris twitters like a scolding bird, that's the signal that it is annoyed! To avoid danger, a slow loris will back its way up a tree, step by step.

Primates can be divided into four groups—prosimians, New World monkeys, Old World monkeys, and the great apes. Humans belong to the same group as apes. Primatologists (scientists who study primates) believe both humans and apes shared a common ancestor about 20 million years ago.

What was the original primate ancestor like? By studying existing prosimians and ancient fossils, primatologists are getting a pretty clear picture.

PRIMATES

Philippine Tarsier (*Tarsius syrichta*)

What is forty million years old, has huge saucer eyes, a hairy nose, and pop eyes in the back of its head? What else? A tiny tarsier.

Actually, a tarsier's eyes are located on either side of its nose, just like human eyes.

But tarsiers can swivel their necks 180 degrees so they can see who's sneaking up from behind. Gotcha!

These mighty mini-animals are among the smallest of all monkey species. They weigh about 4½ ounces, about the size of a guinea pig. Babies are mouse-sized, and they cling to their mothers from birth, chirping noisily. When they're in a hurry, mothers also carry their babies by mouth, just like cats do, or they plop them on a handy branch when they go hunting.

Tarsiers are mighty leapers and can jump from tree to tree in the tropical forests of Southeast Asia where they live. Grown-up tarsiers can leap long distances and land on their two hind feet. In midair, they keep arms and legs close to their bodies and use their tails to steer. When they come down to earth, tarsiers leap like frogs.

When they're not jumping, they're often grooming fellow tarsiers. For primates, grooming means more than removing ticks, mites, and dirt. It's a way of learning who's who in the social order of a primate group.

When native headhunters of Borneo went on the warpath, it was bad luck to spot a tarsier. Hunters believed it meant they would lose their own heads because tarsiers can swivel theirs.

When tarsiers are excited, their big ears don't stop moving. In fact, they move in two directions at once: while one ear turns forward, the other turns back.

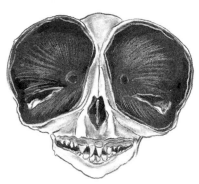

Tarsier eyes are largest in proportion to their body size of all primates. If human eyes were proportionately as pop-eyed, we would be looking at the world through grapefruits!

Jumbo eyes! Each eye is about the same size as the tarsier's brain. They use their big eyes to hunt insects and lizards at night. These are the only primates who restrict their diet to live prey.

Photo, facing page, © Zoological Society of San Diego, photo by Ron Garrison

PRIMATES

Pygmy Marmoset (*Callithrix pygmaea*)

Tucked among tree branches in the forests of the upper Amazon, the olive-colored pygmy marmoset sounds a lot like a bird when it chirrups, twitters, and chik-chiks. There are six to eight types of marmosets—in a variety of colors and sizes. Some have naked faces in gold or black, some have great moustaches, and others sport fuzzy beards. Marmosets are agile monkeys, and they have claws instead of nails on the ends of their fingers. These claws give them a no-slip grip on branches.

Some marmosets grow as large as hefty rats and fat cats, but the pygmy marmoset, only 3 ounces when fully grown, is as small as the mouse lemur. Like all marmosets, pygmies are diurnal, which means they rise and shine with the sun. They spend lots of their day socializing with other pygmy marmosets. They are brave little critters, but they don't look for a fight. If something makes them nervous, they might scurry up the nearest tree like a squirrel. And if they're really scared, their hair stands straight up on their heads.

When a prosimian wants to reach out and catch something, it doesn't have an easy task. Prosimians can move their fingers and toes easily, but all five digits move together. If one finger grabs, they all grab. This is called "whole-hand control." Think about that the next time you try to thread a needle or play a guitar.

Through evolution, primates became better equipped for life in trees. They needed sharp eyes for spying fruit and more brain space to remember where and when it would be ripe. Instead of eyes on the sides of their heads (like horses), primate eyes slowly moved forward for 3-D vision. Areas of the brain devoted to vision and memory got bigger, while smelling centers did not. Just try smelling your way around your house!

PRIMATES

White-faced Saki *(Pithecia pithecia)*

The dot-eyed white-faced saki wears a woebegone expression under its shaggy hood of hair. This shy and sensitive New World monkey makes its home in the highest trees of South American forests. There, it can stride along thin branches like a tightrope walker, standing tall, hands held out for balance, and fingers spread. A saki is quickest when it moves on all fours and leaps from branch to branch.

If sakis stand on two feet and shake their fur, watch out. That's a good sign these monkeys are upset.

When it's time to sleep at night, white-faced sakis curl up like cats among the branches. To reach fruit, berries, and leaves, some types of sakis hang by their hind feet and munch contentedly.

Sakis come with a few variations: there are very hairy ones, and some with beards and red noses. These are animals who need plenty of space, privacy, and trees.

Sakis don't mind getting their feet wet, but their beard is another matter. To drink from streams, sakis often dip their hands into water and then lick their wet fur.

New World monkeys live in South and Central America. Some have prehensile tails that can reach and grab like a third arm. None have tough "sitting pads" on their rear ends like Old World monkeys.

PRIMATES

Weird Wah-CAR-ee!

White Uakari *(Cacajao calvus)*

With naked pink faces and ears, stumpy tails, and wispy hair, uakaris are the weirdest of the weird-looking. Large troops of uakaris roam the branches of the Brazilian rain forest where they spend almost all their time. When the rainy season floods the jungle floor, they don't even touch ground to gather fallen fruits. These cat-sized animals are the only short-tailed monkeys in the Americas. Although their six-inch tails aren't very impressive, uakaris do have long, furry fingers and toes.

Uakaris are often quiet, but they can communicate with loud, hysterical-sounding shrieks, almost as if they're laughing. They are playful, like many monkeys, and the young make up games to amuse themselves.

At one time, native hunters in South American rain forests used blow darts, poisoned with the mucous of frogs, to catch uakaris. When the dart struck its target, the monkeys were paralyzed and fell from the trees. Hunters would sometimes use salt to counteract the poison. Baby uakaris were often kept as pets, but adults were eaten.

In the Middle Ages, physicians dissected the bodies of monkeys so they could learn more about human anatomy. In those days, dissecting a human body for medical purposes was strictly against the rules.

Captive primates can be more aggressive than their relatives in the wild. That's because they are forced to live in small spaces and compete for food. Human primates in big cities are usually more aggressive and grumpy than their country cousins.

PRIMATES

Photo, facing page. © Zoological Society of San Diego

Monkey Business

Black-handed Spider Monkey *(Ateles geoffroyi)*

Spider monkeys, who are found in southern Mexico, through Colombia, Venezuela, and the Amazon Basin, are swinging superstars able to travel in jungle treetops using sure-grip fingers and toes, long arms and legs, and a grabby tail. Spider monkey tails are prehensile, a fancy word for grasping that rhymes with "utensil." Tails come in handy to keep monkeys from falling out of trees when they're asleep. They also keep food and other monkeys within a tail's length, which is longer than an arm's length.

Black-faced, with flesh-colored goggles and white-rimmed eyes, spider monkeys travel in troops of up to 25 individuals. During the day, they search for fresh fruit and nuts. These monkeys are very picky about the fruit they eat. They pinch, sniff, and taste the goods just like some very particular human shoppers.

Spider monkeys must always be on the alert for hungry predators like eagles and jaguars. When threatened, they will scratch their fur nervously and bark like a dog. They will also break off branches (some weighing as much as 10 pounds) and drop them on whoever lurks below.

What's in a name? Spider monkeys are so named because of their long spidery limbs and tail. Also, their knobby joints stick up when they're scurrying along branches so they resemble arachnids with five legs instead of eight!

A spider monkey's tail is so sensitive, it can pick up a peanut.

When rain forest natives went hunting with poison darts, many spider monkeys didn't fall out of trees after they were shot. That's because they were so firmly attached to branches by hands, feet, and tail.

PRIMATES

DeBrazza's Guenon *(Cercopithecus neglectus)*

Spiked, buzzed, and streaked, guenons are some of the flashiest and punkiest monkeys in Africa! They use their colorful faces, as well as head movements, to spot their own kind and to communicate. An up-and-down jerk of the head may mean keep away, while a yawn says, "I'm the boss." Guenons send messages in living color, too. One type of guenon sports a blue mask around its eyes. When it gets excited, the mask turns even bluer—because there's more blood circulating. Of course, humans change colors, too. Some people turn very pink when they're embarrassed.

Guenon monkeys come in a rainbow of colorful designs. Some have blue bottoms, red stripes, red ears, and speckled fur. Others are green with red tails. Or wear yellow whiskers or a white oval nose spot. Some have beards, and others have great tufts of hair on their heads.

With puffy cheeks, white chin whiskers, a white upper lip and throat, an orange-patched forehead, a black mane, and black arms and legs, the DeBrazza's are the most colorful of all guenon monkeys. They gallop on all fours, with their tails held proudly in the air like flags. These fruit, nut, and insect gourmets live in the rain forests of the African Congo.

Thumbs up! DeBrazza's babies suck their thumbs just like human babies.

Guenons spend much of their time in a forest of trees, leaping limb to limb. But they do come down to earth to search for jumpy critters like crickets and grasshoppers, their favorite snack.

Old World monkeys, like the guenons, live in Africa, Southeast Asia, and the Malay Archipelago. They have tough pads (like calluses) on their rumps so they can sleep sitting up in trees.

PRIMATES

206

Patas Monkey (*Erythrocebus patas*)

Troops of muscular, long-legged, red-haired patas monkeys roam the grasslands and deserts of equatorial Africa searching for food—leaves, roots, fruit, insects, beans, seeds, lizards, young birds, and eggs.

Female patas monkeys grow to be 1½ feet tall. These little she-monkeys act as leaders of the troop when the males are busy watching for predators. Adult males are twice as big as females, and one of them always has the job of troop "watch monkey." Other bachelor males travel in their own groups separate from the main troop.

Patas monkeys are not aggressive fighters, and they don't organize against their enemies. When they're threatened, they often crouch down in tall grasses to hide. Sometimes the males will run away to lead predators away from females and baby monkeys.

Nonhuman primates all over the world are threatened by loss of habitat. When humans move into forests, grasslands, and onto mountains, wild creatures must move out. Since we share a very small planet, our primate relatives are running out of living space. Eventually, we humans will face the same problem unless we slow down our population growth.

Three amazing female primates have spent much of their lives learning about great apes. Jane Goodall studies chimpanzees in Tanzania. Birute Galdikas observes orangutans in Borneo. The late Dian Fossey fought to save the mountain gorillas of Rwanda. They all share a deep love for, and commitment to, the great apes.

PRIMATES

Sulawesi Crested Macaque *(Macaca nigra)*

On the Indonesian island of Sulawesi, 10-pound to 25-pound monkeys the color of ebony, with crested hair and pink padded rumps, raise their families peacefully.

At first glance, it's easy to mistake a crested macaque for a baboon. They both walk on all fours, and their pointy skulls are shaped with the same thick protruding eyebrows. But crested macaques are quieter and more easygoing than their baboon relatives.

No one is really sure how the crested macaque first came to the island of Sulawesi. Some say they traveled from the Philippines long, long ago. Now, the crested macaque has only one home, Sulawesi.

To see how important opposable thumbs are, try climbing a tree or picking fruit without using your thumbs!

Some native tribes on Sulawesi worship the crested macaque because they believe these primates are their ancestors. When they fill river rafts with food and set them adrift, they are paying homage to the gods of the apes.

Sulawesi crested macaques look a little like cone heads. As these primates grow older, their hair stands straighter and pointier. If they get excited, it really stands up!

PRIMATES

Gelada *(Theropithecus gelada)*

Rough, tough, and hefty, geladas are fierce troopers. The ruff of hair around an adult male's shoulders makes him look even tougher and heftier than his 45 to 60 pounds of muscle. Since these monkeys have come down from the trees to spend most of their lives on the ground, they have developed new ways to defend themselves from predators like lions, hyenas, and especially leopards.

Long teeth, strong jaws, and powerful shoulder muscles provide protection, and organized group defense gives them power in numbers against any common enemy except humans. Geladas have thick lustrous coats and naked bright red chests. They live at high elevations where food is scarce. Most of their diet consists of grass, roots and all. But they also eat seeds, leaves, onions, and occasional insects—almost anything they can find. Geladas are formidable fighters. To ward off enemies, they will throw stones or roll rocks downhill. Geladas are not fond of their relatives, hamadryas baboons.

Primates are amazingly strong. A 45-pound gelada male has the strength of a human male who is three to six times bigger!

Baboons are close relatives of geladas. Baboons love babies—anybody's! Adults in the troop act as grandparents, aunts, and uncles, sharing food, grooming fur, and cuddling babies in their laps.

Baboon babies have it made in the shade! While grown-up baboons go off to hunt for food, baboon babies spend their time up a tree swinging, climbing, and monkeying around. A few older baboon "baby-sitters" stay behind to look after things. The tree not only makes a great jungle gym to play on but it also keeps babies off the ground and safe from hungry predators.

PRIMATES

In Hot Water

Japanese Macaque or Snow Monkey (*Macaca fuscata*)

Shy snow monkeys go to great depths to stay warm. They spend winter hours soaking in thermal hot springs located in the mountain forests of Japan where they live. In these steamy natural pools, they continue daily life, nursing their babies, grooming, and schooling.

Shaggy, long fur coats help keep snow monkeys warm when they're not in hot water, and cheek pouches are handy for storing food. These macaques sleep in trees at night and wander in search of shoots, buds, and roots during the day. They travel in troops of 30 to 150 members. When they stop to feed, they form two circles. Young male snow monkeys stay on the outer circle. They are the first line of defense against predators. Females, babies, and adult males of high social rank form the inner circle. A dominant male is the most powerful member of the troop. When young monkeys wrestle, play tag, and roughhouse with each other, they also learn their place in the social order.

Japanese scientists spent many years studying snow monkeys. They found these primates use as many as 30 different sounds to communicate with each other. They also watched as snow monkeys learned to do new things. Swimming, for instance. Scientists used peanuts to encourage a few monkeys to go into the ocean. Soon, the snow monkeys had learned to swim and even dive!

One day, a young female snow monkey dipped a sandy sweet potato in water and decided it tasted better clean. A month later, one of her friends washed a sweet potato. Four years later, 15 monkeys were washing potatoes. Nine years later, half of the snow monkeys were doing the same! That's probably how humans learned to wash potatoes thousands of years ago—from the younger generation.

Snow monkeys are part of Japanese art, folklore, and myth. They are the three monkeys who "see no evil, hear no evil, and speak no evil," representing the wisdom of Buddha.

PRIMATES

Mandrill (*Mandrillus sphinx*)

A red nose, bright blue cheeks, a yellow beard and shoulder ruff, and a purply-red rear end are a male mandrill's everyday colors. These dog-faced forest monkeys from western Central Africa reach heights of 2½ feet and weigh in at 55 pounds, and their large bodies are packed with muscle. When provoked, mandrills are as strong as gorillas or leopards.

You can't miss an angry mandrill. His rainbow face turns even brighter colors when more blood circulates, and he yawns to show off four-inch yellow fangs.

When most monkeys show their teeth, watch out! A grin or grimace equals fear in mandrill language. It's easy to believe those fangs are less than friendly.

Ants, beetles, and other insects are mandrill delicacies, and fruits and vegetables are staples. But when they're really hungry, almost anything will do.

Female mandrills and their babies hang out in trees, while male mandrills spend most of their day on the ground. In battle—fighting predators or rival males—mandrills are ferocious, but they can also be gentle and affectionate with each other.

Troops of mandrills, like baboons, maintain a definite hierarchy, or power structure. Chief males spend most of their time with chief females. Their offspring usually inherit their favored positions in mandrill society. Less powerful mandrills act in more submissive roles.

Mandrills walk on all twenty—fingers and toes, that is. They never let the palms of their hands or feet touch the ground.

PRIMATES

Proboscis Monkey (*Nasalis larvatus*)

Honk kee-honk, Cyrano of the swampy Borneo rain forest has arrived! Male proboscis monkeys sport a schnozz that just won't stop—growing, that is. If a proboscis monkey is lucky, his nose will grow to lengths of four inches—so long, it overhangs his mouth. To female monkeys, the longer the male's nose, the stronger the sex appeal.

Proboscis monkeys grow to be as tall as 2½ feet from head to toe, and they may weigh as much as 50 pounds. They honk (males kee-honk) when they're happily eating leaves, shoots, and assorted fruits or catching sun rays. To relax or nap, they stretch out on their backs. Baby proboscis monkeys like to spend their play time swinging from grown-up tails or squeezing the biggest nose that's handy.

Proboscis monkeys live in very flexible social groups. The button-eyed male proboscis monkeys are famous for their grand noses and pinkish brown faces, but all babies begin life with small noses and deep blue faces.

Proboscis monkeys get their name from a Latin word for an elephant's trunk. Their noses are fleshy and flexible, and some are so long, they get in the way when these animals eat or drink.

Proboscis monkeys love to get into the swim. They high-dive 50 feet from trees, swim under water, and dogpaddle across streams, lakes, and even oceans. Waterlogged proboscis monkeys have been rescued far from ocean shores by fishing boats.

The nose of the male proboscis monkey keeps growing its entire life. Because females prefer to mate with the longest-nosed males, evolution ensures that proboscis monkeys will remain Cyrano of the rain forest.

Photo, facing page, courtesy Animals Animals © M. Austerman

PRIMATES

What's the Drill?

Drill (*Mandrillus leucophaeus*)

Drills, like their close relatives the mandrills, will eat almost anything. A drill smorgasbord includes roots, fruit, plants, snails, lizards, insects, mice, snakes, frogs, and worms for dessert!

When troops of five to fifty drills are wandering among the trees of a forest, they like to stay in constant contact with each other. To do this, they keep up steady grunting and snorting noises. Even if they can't be seen, they're heard! Drills also chatter and make faces when they're flustered. If they're really upset, they may run around shrieking.

When a 60-pound drill gives a friendly shake of the head and shoulders, that's a request to be groomed. Hopefully, another drill will carefully remove bugs, ticks, and mites from its fur. When grooming others, a drill will press its teeth together and make loud smacking noises of satisfaction. A small smile with chattering teeth is a friendly greeting that says, "I feel good."

Angry drills and mandrills are easy to spot. They slap the ground with one hand while the hair on their neck stands up. The colored areas on their bodies turn even brighter. They never take their eyes from whoever is upsetting them. They also spread their arms, lower their heads, and flash their powerful teeth in a big yawn. This is called "threat posture." It's a way of telling someone, "Watch out, I'm warning you!" After giving this behavior several tries, these animals may sit down and scratch their arms and thighs energetically. Or, they may attack!

Drills and mandrills are known to live as long as forty years, maybe more!

Ancient Egyptians trained hamadryas baboons to do their simple chores like collecting firewood and harvesting cultivated figs. They also worshiped the "smartest" of these baboons, giving them special tasks to perform in temples. Some were even mummified and buried with pharaohs.

Have you ever seen a snail playing? Probably not. Playing around is something only mammals seem to do. We humans play a lot, especially when we're young. And so do primates! Just watch a baby chimpanzee, baboon, or gorilla.

PRIMATES

Lowland Gorilla (Gorilla gorilla gorilla)

These gentle giants from Africa can reach a height of more than 5 feet, and one 300-pound gorilla may be as strong as 10 humans. But gorillas are not the "monsters" that run rampant on the late-late show. In fact, unless gorillas think their families are in danger, they are very peaceable.

Gorillas live in small groups, and they often mingle peacefully with other gorilla families. When a male gorilla is between 11 and 13 years old, he grows silver hairs on his back. This silver-back can then become the leader of his own family group. When he wants to scare off intruders or remind his family who's the boss, the silver-back begins by screaming, then bites a leaf between his lips. Standing on his hind legs, tossing twigs into the air, he beats his great chest. For a finale, he tears out grass and plants, runs around on all fours, and beats the floor with his hand. (If that seems strange, just watch a human primate on the dance floor.)

Gorillas have been tested for intelligence by human standards. Some are as "smart" as human kids. Gorillas certainly do lots of "people" things—or maybe people do lots of "gorilla" things. They clean their ears and pick their noses with their index fingers. They yawn, burp, hiccough, scratch, and huff and puff. Mothers kiss babies, and babies climb onto their father's lap. They use at least 22 sounds to communicate with each other.

Gorillas are rare and endangered because humans are moving into their homeland. Also, poachers often kill entire gorilla families in order to capture one baby. Although gorillas (and other great apes) are not human, many people believe that killing them is murder. These people are working hard to make sure great apes will not become extinct.

Gorillas are known to catch small animals like lizards and frogs in the wild and "pet" them gently.

Gorillas are complete vegetarians. They not only eat plants, they also wear big leaves on their heads as decoration.

One of a gorilla's favorite treats is wild celery.

Besides 10,000 lowland gorillas, there are less than 350 mountain gorillas left on earth. These primates live in a small area of Africa called the Virunga Volcano region. Many conservation groups are working hard to protect these gorillas from poachers and to provide money for primate research. But we must hurry!

PRIMATES

Photo, facing page, © Zoological Society of San Diego, photo by Ron Garrison

Chuckwalla *(Sauromalus obesus)*

All reptiles are *ecto-thermic* animals, that is, they depend on their outside environment for body heat. Another thing reptiles have in common with each other are backbones, which is why they're known as vertebrates. They also breathe air, lay shelled eggs, and have scales.

More than 250 million years ago, reptiles first crept out of the shallow seas and ventured on land. Of course, the land-lubbing process was gradual. First, reptiles had to develop legs, lungs, scaly skins, and shelled eggs. But the evolutionary effort was worth it; on land, there were plenty of insects to eat and dense forests for shelter. Lizards, turtles, snakes, crocodilians, and the rare tuatara are the five groups of reptiles found on Earth today.

The lizard known as the chuckwalla is blessed with skin as rough, tough, and grainy as sandpaper. Like the desert iguana, the "chuck" needs lots of solar heat to keep its flat, broad body warm and spends much of its day soaking up warmth from rocks and stones in the desert Southwest. When chuckwallas reach old age, and their heaviest weight, they waddle slowly from rock to burrow.

There are about 3,000 species of lizards in the world. They range in size from 1½ inches long to 18 feet! Geckos, skinks, and iguanas are lizards. So is the chameleon.

At the slightest hint of danger, a "chuck" will crawl into a small rock crevice and lock itself in by swelling up its body. Once "anchored," a chuckwalla is almost impossible to move.

There are only two living species of tuataras, or "beak headed" reptiles. Long ago, many different types of these animals flourished on Earth. Today, tuataras are found only on the small islands of New Zealand. Scientists believe tuataras sometimes live as long as 125 years!

Two hundred million years ago, dinosaurs first appeared on earth. Were they reptiles? Although their name comes from two Greek words meaning "terrible lizard," many scientists believe dinosaurs belong to their own class, Dinosauria. In the year 2525, this question will probably still be a question because there are no dinosaurs around to answer it.

REPTILES

Marine Iguana (*Amblyrhynchus cristatus*)

Marine iguanas live on the Galápagos Islands (off the coast of Ecuador) where they spend much of their day sunning on warm boulders. These animals, who thrive on a diet of seaweed and algae, are the only lizards in the world that feed in salt water. When they swim out to eat, they take great bites of seaweed from ocean rocks using both sides of their jaws—like a dog gnawing on a bone.

Many iguanas have very unusual helmets, or crests, on their heads and a variety of flaps and wrinkles at their throats. Marine iguanas are no exception: they have a mane of rubbery spikes running along their upper backs to the top of their dragonlike heads as well as double or triple chins. When they are trying to frighten off predators or other lizards, they show off their headgear.

Although they're not exactly graceful on land, marine iguanas swim with ease and move through the water quickly. They tuck their legs close to their bodies and move their tails like a large snake.

When naturalist Charles Darwin visited the Galápagos Islands in 1835, he found that both land and marine iguanas had no fear of humans. Since that time, humans have hunted iguanas until very few are left. Now, sadly, these amazing creatures are in danger of extinction.

Many scientists visit the Galápagos Islands because it is such a special world. The animals on these islands evolved in ways that are unique. Sadly, these days, the creatures of the Galápagos are endangered by human activity, just like animals everywhere.

Iguanas come in assorted sizes—4 inches to 7 feet—and they are the most common lizards in Central and South America. But iguanas also live in North America, the West Indies, Madagascar, and the Fiji Islands. In all, there are about 700 species of iguanas in the world.

Photo, facing page, © James P. Rowan

REPTILES

Siamese Crocodile *(Crocodylus siamensis)*

Crocodiles, alligators, and gharials all belong to the reptile group known as crocodilians. These armored and prehistoric-looking creatures are the biggest living reptiles. Some species grow more than 25 feet long! They're also the reptiles most closely related to the ancient dinosaurs.

But don't let all that prehistoric armor fool you—crocodilians are very advanced reptiles when it comes to their hearts. On land, or a nose above water, crocodilians breathe air just like humans. Their heart works like a mammal's four-chambered heart. Used blood is pumped from the body to the heart and finally to the lungs. Refreshed with oxygen in the lungs, the blood makes a return trip—from lungs to heart to body. But when they are submerged in water and holding their breath, crocodilians depend on their reptile hearts. A valve separating the heart chambers opens. Used blood mixes with fresh blood and gets recyled over and over until all the air is used up. Then crocodilians must surface and breathe again—using a four-chambered heart.

Crocodilians are great swimmers and nifty cruisers. Keeping their legs folded close to the body, they whiplash the water with their thick tails. Just like human swimmers, they can kick off the bottom with their hind legs for quick spurts and turns. Crocodiles float in river currents with only their bulging eyes, ears, and nostrils above water. Swimming birds, turtles, and fishes disappear with a snap of the jaws. Even land animals dipping their noses into the water for a drink can be pulled from shore by the powerful grip of crocodile jaws.

Small birds pick parasites off the bodies of one species of crocodilians, the Nile crocodile. They even rush to meet crocs as they emerge from the water. Since they're doing crocodiles a favor, they don't get eaten!

Some species of crocodiles can swim in salt water, and they sometimes travel great ocean distances. Saltwater crocs can grow to lengths of 16 feet, and the record is 32 feet!

Large crocodilians usually spend their nights in water and their days lazing in the sun. To stay cool in midday, they lie with mouths open wide. Like panting dogs, they cool by evaporation.

Mugger crocodiles are believed to be sacred in some parts of India. At a famous crocodile pool in Pakistan, religious pilgrims pay their respects to more than 50 crocodiles who are considered to be priests.

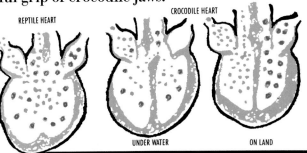

MAMMAL HEART

REPTILE HEART

CROCODILE HEART

UNDER WATER

ON LAND

REPTILES

Komodo Dragon (*Varanus komodoensis*)

Reaching a length of 10 feet and a weight of 250 pounds, thickly armored and ancient-looking Komodo dragons are one of the the world's largest lizards.

Although Komodo bodies are big, their territory is small. In the wild, they can only be found on Komodo and a few other small islands in Indonesia.

Komodo dragons are flesh eaters. They prey on small wild deer, pigs, and domestic animals. They also work as nature's scavengers, eating the remains of dead animals.

Like all monitor lizards, Komodos have long necks, heavy bodies, and thick tails. They are also equipped with dangerous-looking claws. They use these sharp claws and their equally sharp teeth for tearing their prey into bite-sized chunks. Using a little imagination, Komodos really do look like magnificent dragons.

What's your "habitat"? Since habitat is the place you naturally live, yours might be New York, Detroit, or Amarillo. Komodo dragons have a very limited habitat of a few islands in Indonesia; unlike you, they do not survive anywhere else.

Komodo dragons are big, but another lizard, Salvador's monitor (*Varanus salvadori*), is biggest, reaching lengths of more than 18 feet!

230

REPTILES

Spiny Softshell Turtle *(Trionyx spiniferus)*

Turtles are known for their thick armored shells, some of which can support more than 200 times their weight. But softshell turtles are just that; they have to rely on a rubbery shell of skin that has tough cartilage, or gristle, around the edges. Their shells have lost those tough horny plates common to their hard-shelled relatives.

The spiny softshell turtle of North America grows to a length of 18 inches and sports a snorkel-snout for a nose. This "snorkel" acts as a breathing tube for the spiny softshell, who lives completely in water. Spiny softshells can also be found in parts of Asia and Africa. Fossils prove that this turtle also wandered through what is now Europe 65 million years ago.

Although turtles have a reputation for slow going, the spiny softshell is often an active creature. It makes up for its lack of hard-shelled armor by biting and scratching with clawed front feet when it's handled. This softshell is called "spiny" because of the tiny leathery spines covering its back.

Cartoon turtles may be able to leave their shells behind, but real turtles can't! Just like you have a skeleton that stays inside your skin, a turtle's shell protects its soft body for life. The upper shell of a turtle is called the *carapace*. The lower shell protecting the turtle's belly is the *plastron*.

REPTILES

A Swell Head

Helmeted Lizard *(Corytophanes cristatus)*

Lizards try a variety of ways to ward off enemies. Some come in colors designed to blend in with the background so they can't be seen. Some leave their tails (or patches of skin) behind to confuse predators while they make their getaway. Others use a special threat display that makes them look big, bigger, biggest! The aim is to look too huge and fierce to tangle with.

For the helmeted lizard, threat posture means the bony "helmet" on the back of its head raises and the skin on its neck swells up. The result is an enormous head. But that's not the end of looking scary. This lizard lifts itself tall on its legs, turns sideways, and its eyes bulge out fiercely. For a final touch, it tips its head down to reveal its helmet.

We humans have our own "threat displays." Have you ever watched a human make a weird face, swell up his or her chest, raise a fist, or swagger down the street? Those are all ways of saying, "Don't mess with me!"

Which came first, the reptile or the egg? Shelled eggs might make you think of chickens and other birds, but really, the first shelled eggs on land were reptilian!

Mexico's two-legged wriggly worm lizard, the ajolote (ah-hoe-LOW-tay), is one of the rarest reptiles in the Western Hemisphere. This lizard uses its two tiny legs (they're only as long as 1/20th of its body length) to burrow into dry, hard ground. When the ajolote is digging into soft ground, its blunt head serves as a bulldozer. It may look like a worm, but it's really a lizard!

REPTILES

Plumed Basilisk *(Basiliscus plumifrons)*

In the rain forests of Central America lives a very distinguished lizard—the basilisk; it can run on water. For this reason, the basilisk is known by local people as the Jesus Christ lizard. Speedy basilisks have been clocked at speeds of 12 kilometers per hour as they whizz across land or water. Because their toes are widened with skin and they run on their two hind legs at such speeds, they don't have time to sink! They are also moving too fast to be caught by aquatic predators.

Basilisks can start their run across water in three ways. They can begin on land, jump onto water from a branch, or rise to the water's surface. You might call them the triathletes of the lizard world.

But basilisks are not content to skim the waves; they also hang out underwater. They are super swimmers and excellent divers, and they can stay on the bottom of a lake or steam for as long as 30 minutes. That's a nifty way to avoid predators on land.

Mythical monster? No, a basilisk. This little lizard is named for a mythical Greek monster who was half rooster and half snake. Supposedly, the monster's looks could kill by turning you to stone!

The skinny! Lizards (and other reptiles) shed their skin at regular intervals. Large flakes and pieces fall off, and a shiny new skin is already underneath. This process is called molting.

REPTILES

CHAK

Northern Leaf-tailed Gecko *(Phyllurus cornutus)*

With more than 800 different types of geckos spread far and wide over the warm areas of the Earth, these lizards are worldly creatures. Although some species of geckos are silent, their name comes from the "geck-oh" sound that others make.

The northern leaf-tailed gecko has a tail that looks like a leaf. In fact, its head looks like a leaf, too. Its entire body is designed to act as camouflage so it blends in with the background. That way, snakes, birds, cats, and other predators can't see the lizard for the leaf—hopefully!

Another way the leaf-tailed gecko uses its head to protect itself is by using its thick, stumpy tail. Since both ends of this gecko look alike, a hungry predator can hardly tell if the leaf-tailed gecko is coming or going.

Noisy! Some geckos are commonly named for the noises they make. Geckos use their tongues and mouths to "geck," "toke," and "chak." That's why you'll find geckos named "tokay" and "cheekchak."

FOOD?

Good-luck geckos! Many folks in Asia believe the "geck" of a gecko brings great fortune (and leaves behind fewer cockroaches, too).

Get a good look at a gecko—the holes behind the eyes are ears!

REPTILES

Photo, facing page, courtesy Animals Animals © Klaus Uhlenhut

Frilled Lizard *(Chlamydosaurus kingi)*

The Australian frilled lizard is famous for its extremely impressive and scaly neck frill. Usually this frill lies like folds of fabric against the lizard's body. But when the frilled lizard feels threatened, it's a different story. If this lizard tightens the muscles connected to its tongue bones, the frill fans out like a great umbrella. The view of a lizard with open mouth and raised frill can be a very threatening sight for would-be predators. That's why this is called a threat posture.

Frilled lizards spend most of their time in trees eating insects. When they do come down to the ground, they run quickly on two hind legs. Frilled lizard tracks look more like bird tracks—only three out of four toes show up.

One relative of the frilled lizard's is the water lizard from the East Indies and New Guinea. These "giants" grow more than 3 feet long.

Another relative, a small lizard called the draco, is known for its flying powers. These animals from Asia and the East Indies have scaly membranes (or "wings") on the sides of their bodies which extend from front to back legs. Dracos glide from tree to tree using their wings to guide them.

REPTILES

Photo, facing page, courtesy Animals Animals © Klaus Uhlenhut

Northern Snake-necked Turtle *(Chelodina rugosa)*

With a neck that stretches out like a snake and lots of loose wrinkly skin around its shoulders, the northern snake-necked turtle from Australia won't win any beauty contests. But a turtle's survival success is based on its ability to find food, defend itself, and produce more turtles—not beauty! These swift, nimble, and snappish critters capture small fish with a snakelike forward dart of the neck.

Of course, the snake-necked turtle has an extra-long neck to protect. This animal, also known as the side-necked turtle, has to bend its neck sideways to hide its head under its shell.

Many humans hunt turtles (and turtle eggs), killing so many that some species have become endangered. But humans have also worshiped turtles for millions of years. Stone Age people left behind small carvings of turtles. Greek legends tell the story of the god Apollo inventing the lyre by tying strings across a sea turtle's shell. African myths speak of a very clever turtle. And for Indians in South America, the turtle is beloved.

Turtles are the only toothless reptiles. But watch out for your tootsies! Hooked beaks and sharp-edged mouths give turtles plenty of bite.

Good sense! Three of a turtle's senses—sight, smell, and touch—are highly developed.

COOL   WARM

INCUBATION

Weather or not—male or female? For a number of turtles, the sex of their young seems to be decided by temperature. Warm or cool incubation could mean all male or all female youngsters. Fortunately for both sexes, the weather is always changing!

REPTILES

Armadillo Lizard (*Cordylus cataphractus*)

The South African armadillo lizard is named for its tough coat of protective scales that look as thick as medieval armor. This slow creature grows to a length of six inches and is especially equipped to defend itself. When threatened, the armadillo lizard puts its tail in its mouth and rolls into a tight ball. This way, predators may get a mouthful of spiny skin, but the lizard's soft belly is protected. The armadillo's layered scales are so thick, they seem as hard as rocks—and not very tasty!

Armadillo lizards are active during the day and spend their time on the ground. Dry ground at that! These animals are found in desert habitats. They can't afford to be particular about how hot it gets or what they eat, and they're not. Over centuries, they've evolved for a perfect fit.

Another armored lizard, the horned toad, lives in North America. When battling with canine or feline predators, this horny creature will squirt jets of blood from its eyes. That could mean a surprise for your cat or dog.

Like horned toads, thorny devils from Australia are ant gourmets. When they find an ant trail, they'll sit and devour the insects for hours.

REPTILES

Photo, facing page, courtesy Animals Animals © Zig Leszczynski

Shingleback Skink (*Trachydosaurus rugosus*)

Skinks come in about 800 species, and they live in the warmer areas of the earth. Although there are many varieties, most skinks are very similar in color, shape, and habit.

The shingleback skink—a.k.a. the pine cone, stump-tail, bobtail, or double-headed lizard—is a dark brown, scaly critter that does have a tail that is short, stumpy, and looks much like its head. Two heads are better than one when a predator is trying to figure out which way a skink will try to run. Also, the fat stored in the skink's tail comes in very handy when food is scarce.

When offered the chance, shinglebacks will eat snails, slugs, ants, small animals, and carcasses—almost anything! They even eat small stones to help digest their food. They are very clean reptiles to have around.

When threatened, shinglebacks have a surprise for their enemies. They hiss and open their mouths to show off their gray blue tongues.

Shinglebacks don't lay eggs. Instead, their babies (usually there are two or three) are born live.

Shinglebacks are called that because the heavy, bony scales on their backs lay over each other just like the shingles on your roof.

Photo facing page courtesy Animals Animals © K. G. Preston Mafham

REPTILES

American Alligator *(Alligator mississippiensis)*

Less than 20 years ago, American alligators had almost disappeared from planet Earth because humans were killing them for their hides, for sport, and to make room for more humans. Now, because of strong laws against poaching and because these animals are hearty, American alligators have returned to many parts of Florida, Louisiana, and nearby states. These reptiles seem to adapt easily to human neighbors.

American alligators have been known to grow more than 19 feet long. But the average size is more like 6 to 12 feet.

Female American alligators are good mothers. They build nests—big enough for several humans to fit inside—of mud and grass and stay close by for several months while eggs incubate. There may be 20 to 70 hardshelled eggs per nest. The mother grunts to her eggs gently, and when the babies are finally ready to hatch, they chirrup back. This way, the female knows it's time to help with the hatching.

Parents of some crocodilians help open eggs and carry babies to water for a bath. Babies stay close to their parents for several years. They are often seen hitching a crocodile-back ride on their parents.

Although they do spend time out of water, crocodilians are clumsier with all four feet on dry land.

American alligator eggs are about as big as a goose egg.

Alligators have not changed much during the 200 million years they've existed on Earth.

Some humans swim with plugs in their ears and noses to keep from getting waterlogged. Crocodilians don't need extra equipment. Valves in their ears and nostrils shut out water below the water line.

GRUNT

CHIRRUP

REPTILES

Vacuum Packed!

South American Matamata Turtle *(Chelus fimbriatus)*

With its flat head, flexible snorkle, and long neck with shaggy flaps of skin, the mata-mata turtle is probably one of the weirdest-look-ing of all reptiles. Its body resembles a pile of muck and leaves. But weird looks are no hardship for the matamata —instead, it's great camouflage. To small fish and aquatic animals, this turtle's fringed and lumpy body must seem like something good to nib-ble on. When fish swim too close, watch out! The matamata's head shoots out, its rubbery jaws and throat open wide, and water— containing any nearby food—is sucked inside like dust into a vacuum cleaner.

The matamata is a very quiet turtle. In fact, you'd hardly know it's around. It is most active at twilight and after dark. Like crocodiles, the back of the matamata's eyes have a crystalline lining that reflects light. It gives these turtle eyes an eerie gleam.

The alligator snapper is a turtle with a twist. In muddy water, it looks like part of the river or lake bottom. There it waits, jaws open. If you could see inside its mouth, you'd see a built-in "worm." This bait is actually part of the turtle's mouth. When fish swim near, al-ligator snappers wiggle their "worms" enticingly, and then they strike, sure and lightning fast. Snap!

REPTILES

Hasselquist's Gecko (Ptyodactylus hasselquistii)

Some geckos are clingy climbers with feet capable of sticky feats! The bottom of a gecko's toes are designed with clinging pads. A closer look shows these pads are covered with microscopic hairs. These teensy hairs have blunt ends that press against small surface areas and give most geckos "sticky power."  On the move, geckos can climb trees, scale walls, and even cruise on the ceiling with the greatest of ease.

Hasselquist's gecko (a.k.a. "house gecko") has a big head and bulging eyes. This gecko's foot pads are shaped like fans and give it special adhesive powers. Hasselquist's gecko also sports claws at the ends of its toes.

During mating season, male and female pairs of these geckos, who live in Algeria, Central Sahara, Iraq, and Iran, stake out their territory and defend it. Hasselquist's geckos are known to live as long as 10 years.

Besides climbing, some geckos also fly. At least, they glide. With wide flaps of skin on each side of its body and webbed feet, Asiatic forest geckos can glide from tree to tree.

All geckos (except a few species in New Zealand) lay eggs.

Some people believe that geckos are poisonous and dangerous to humans. Wrong! Although a gecko bite might hurt, it won't do any permanent damage.

REPTILES

Photo, facing page, courtesy Animals Animals © Fredrik Ehrenstrom/OSF

GREEN TREE PYTHON (*Chondropython viridis*)

Boas and pythons are giants among snakes. They kill their prey by constriction. Usually an animal is first caught by the snake's teeth. (The green tree python from New Guinea has very big front teeth—the better to grasp startled prey on the run.) Then, almost instantly, the snake coils its body around its victim until it suffocates. Two or three extremely tight coils are usually enough to stop the prey's breathing and heart beat.

Many humans fear snakes, but only four types of constricting snakes can possibly be dangerous to humans. Of those, only the South American anaconda is found in the New World. Anacondas *have* killed humans—but very, very rarely!

A female python keeps her egg clutch warm by shivering. This uses lots of energy, and she may lose as much as half her body weight between egg-laying and hatching. It may take two or three years before she has regained enough of her energy reserves to breed again.

South American anacondas are the world's largest snakes. They have been rumored to reach lengths of 12 meters (about 40 feet), but no one is sure. On the record, reticulated pythons have measured in at lengths of nearly 10 meters (about 33 feet)!

Anacondas and reticulated pythons are both expert swimmers, and the python even swims in saltwater. It was one of the first reptiles to reach Krakatoa (by water) from neighboring Sumatra or Java after the 1888 volcanic eruption which destroyed all life on the tiny island.

Green tree pythons are the color of green leaves. They blend in perfectly with their forest surroundings.

S N A K E S

It's a Strike!

WESTERN DIAMONDBACK RATTLESNAKE (*Crotalus atrox*)

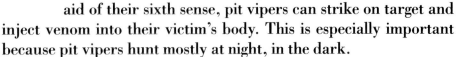

North American rattlesnakes, South American fer-de-lances, and copperheads and moccasins (found in many parts of the world) are all known as pit vipers. Pit vipers are named for their sixth sense, an organ (or pit) that is located between each nostril and each eye. This organ can sense changes in temperature, which allows the snake to detect body heat given off by prey. With the aid of their sixth sense, pit vipers can strike on target and inject venom into their victim's body. This is especially important because pit vipers hunt mostly at night, in the dark.

After a pit viper strikes, its victim usually lives long enough to travel a distance from its predator. How does the snake know where to find its wounded prey? Two internal cavities located near the snake's snout connect to its mouth. These are filled with nerve ends (very much like the ones used for smelling) that enable the snake to trail its victim. Often, snakes with this ability also have a separate and very good sense of smell.

The western diamondback rattlesnake lives in western regions of North America. It grows to a length of more than 2 meters (about 7 feet), and it feeds mostly on rodents.

Water moccasins are pit vipers. They're also the only poisonous water snakes in the United States.

Rattlesnakes are part of Native American myth, medicine, religion, and folklore. The world-famous Hopi Indian snake dance lasts nine days. On the last day, priests actually dance with rattlesnakes. When the dance ends, the snakes are released in the four directions, and their job is to carry a positive message to the rain gods. But don't you try dancing with snakes: viper bites can be fatal.

SNAKES

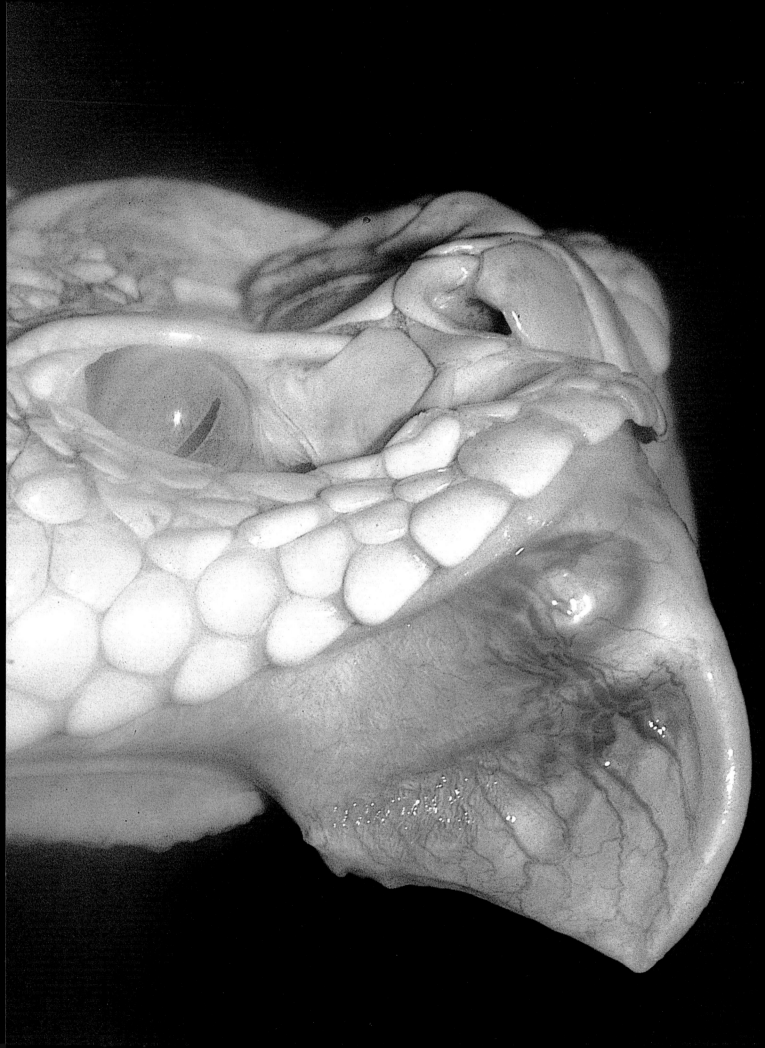

CALIFORNIA KING SNAKE
(*Lampropeltis getula californiae*)

This California king snake is an albino, so it is especially unusual. An albino is any animal (human or otherwise) who lacks pigment; for this reason, it has very white skin and pink eyes. A normal California king snake is one of North America's most colorful snakes—banded or striped, black and yellow.

All king snakes have smooth scales, and they usually grow to a length of three to four feet. Although they eat lizards, frogs, small mammals, and eggs, they also prey on other snakes—even venomous ones. Immunity to snake venom is a characteristic of snake-eating snakes from all continents.

When it hunts, the king snake strikes, wraps its body around its prey, and then kills by constriction the same way giant boas and pythons do. It usually hunts at dawn or dusk.

King snakes are oviparous, which means their young hatch out of eggs. There are usually about ten eggs per clutch (batch). Eastern, speckled, and desert king snakes are close relatives of California king snakes. They live on rocky hillsides and in meadows and woodlands in the southern United States.

Although the Age of Reptiles (which lasted about 120 million years) ended about 70 million years ago, more than 6,500 reptile species exist today, and of those, roughly 3,000 species are snakes. Snakes live almost everywhere in the world except arctic regions.

Although a warm tropical forest is almost always snake country, there are no snakes native to Hawaii.

King snakes earned their name because they prey on venomous snakes.

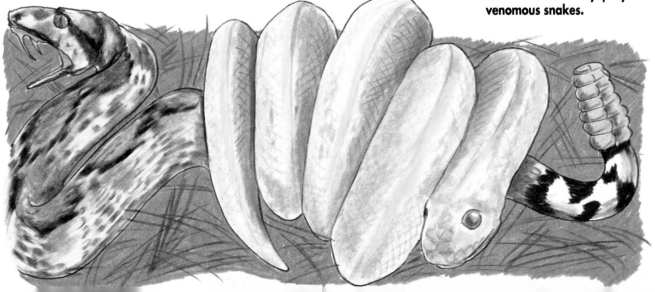

Photo, facing page, Photo Researchers, Inc., courtesy Steinhart Aquarium © Tom McHugh

BLUNT-HEADED TREE SNAKE (*Imantodes cenchoa*)

No doubt about it, blunt-headed tree snakes are weird looking: they have an extremely slim body, a big head, and big eyes. They also do weird things—such as act like an I-beam girder to bridge the gaps between branches where they hang out. Blunt-headed tree snakes will change their shape slightly and stiffen their body to reach a distant branch. Once they firmly attach to the new branch, their body relaxes again.

Blunt-headed tree snakes become active at dusk, and they hunt—for anoles, geckos, and other lizards—during the night. In daylight, they prefer to coil and rest in leaf clumps or in the leaf whorls of bromeliad plants. Several blunt-headed tree snakes may share the same resting place.

Blunt-headed tree snake habitat extends from the forests of southern Mexico to Bolivia and Paraguay. They hatch from eggs, and adults may reach a length of more than 100 centimeters (over 3 feet).

More than 250 million years ago, reptiles first crept out of the shallow seas and ventured on land. The evolutionary effort was worth it; on land, there were plenty of insects to eat and dense forests for shelter. Today, lizards, turtles, snakes, crocodilians, and the rare tuatara are the five groups of reptiles found on earth.

Blunt-headed tree snakes have fangs in the rear of their mouth. They strike their prey swiftly and accurately.

SNAKES

PARROT SNAKE (*Leptophis* sp.)

Parrot snakes—and most other harmless or slightly venomous snakes—belong to the scientific family *Colubridae*. Members of this family range from blunt-headed burrowers to water snakes to long, slender tree dwellers.

Parrot snakes have adapted to life in small trees and shrubs in the forests of southern Mexico, Central America, and South America. They are usually blue-green (like the parrots they are named for), and they forage among the leaves for lizards and frogs, their main prey.

The parrot snake is oviparous, and there are usually four to six eggs per clutch. A newly hatched parrot snake will measure between 25 and 30 centimeters (10 and 12 inches) long, while the adult can be more than 1.20 meters (4 feet) in length.

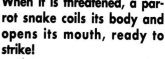

When it is threatened, a parrot snake coils its body and opens its mouth, ready to strike!

Of all reptiles, snakes are probably the most endangered. Loss of habitat (living space) is one of the biggest threats. So is the automobile. Wherever there are roads, snakes are in danger of being run over.

Photo, facing page, Animals Animals © Michael Fogden

S N A K E S

CAT-EYED SNAKE (*Leptodeira* sp.)

Cat-eyed snakes are named for their elliptical (curved), vertical pupils that lend them a catty look. Their pupils admit or shut out light more efficiently than round pupils.

Other senses aid cat-eyed snakes when they are on the prowl. All snakes (and some lizards) have special cells—known as the Jacobson's organ—on the roof of their mouth. The Jacobson's organ helps them "smell" and "taste" with their tongue. A snake's forked tongue picks up chemical particles in the air. When the tongue is flicked around inside the mouth, the particles are transferred to the Jacobson's organ. This ability to taste and smell aids the snake as it detects enemies or as it searches for prey or a mate.

Cat-eyed snakes are both terrestrial and arboreal, which means they spend their time on the ground and in trees. They range from Arizona in the north to Argentina in the south, but most are found in northern South America.

For centuries, snakes have played important roles in literature, religion, and mythology. After all, it was a Biblical serpent who enticed Eve to sample the forbidden fruit. And Shakespeare's Cleopatra poisoned herself with the help of an asp, an Egyptian snake.

Cat-eyed snakes feed on lizards, frogs, and other small animals. The snake in this picture is dining on frog's eggs.

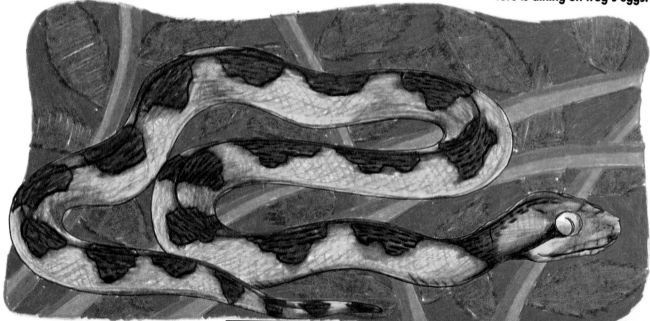

S N A K E S

Second Skin

RED RAT SNAKE (*Elaphe guttata*)

All snakes molt (shed their skin) from time to time, and young snakes molt more frequently. They do this because they need room to grow and also because they need to replace old, worn-out skin.

As a snake's outer skin begins to loosen from the new skin underneath, its eyes become temporarily cloudy—they're covered with skin, too!—and its eyesight dims. For this reason, a molting snake is extremely vulnerable to predators, and it will usually go into hiding until the old skin is completely shed. When a snake molts, it also becomes very touchy and aggressive. A normally harmless snake will bite if it is disturbed.

To molt, this North American red rat snake loosens the old skin around its head and lips and then crawls out of its "wrapper." Although the snake loses its appetite several days before the molt, it returns to its normal activities when its skin is entirely shed.

Rat snakes are terrestrial and arboreal. On their belly, they have a sharp plate that helps them get a grip on bark as they climb trees. They feed on birds and eggs in trees and small mammals in their burrows below ground. Rat snakes kill their prey by constriction.

All snakes lack eyelids. Instead, their eyes are covered by skin cells. Just like the skin on the rest of its body, this thin eye covering is shed when the snake molts.

Molting continues throughout a snake's lifetime. Most reptiles never stop growing, and they need new skin to help protect them from environmental wear and tear and from predators.

A snake's scales are thick segments of skin. They are mostly made of keratin, and they are a lot like your fingernails.

Photo, facing page, Animals Animals © Zig Leszczynski

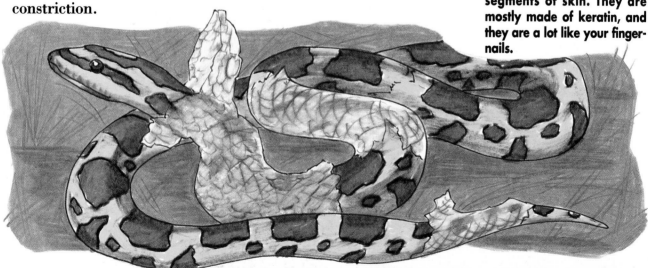

S N A K E S

BLACK-TAILED RATTLESNAKE (*Crotalus molossus*)

In the deserts of the southwestern United States and Mexico, a high-pitched buzz warns passersby that the black-tailed rattlesnake is near.

A rattlesnake's rattle is a signal to larger animals to stay away! If they heed the warning, the snake avoids injury, and so does the horse, deer, cow, human, or whatever creature may be in harm's way.

The rattle consists of a series of hard, horny sections at the end of the snake's tail. Actually, each section is unshed skin, and one is added every time the snake molts.

Newly born rattlesnakes have a prebutton, a large scale at the tip of their tail. The first time young rattlesnakes molt, the prebutton is lost and section number one (the button formed underneath) appears. Several more loose sections must develop before young snakes can really rattle. It is these sections moving against each other when the tail is vibrated that produces the high-pitched sound. Most adult rattlesnakes have no more than eight rattles because those sections at the end of the tail tend to wear down or fall off with age.

Black-tailed rattlesnakes prefer rocky areas, and they are more likely than other rattlesnake species to be active during the day. They may reach a length of about 1.22 meters (4 feet), and they feed mostly on rodents.

There are 29 species of rattlesnakes, and they are all viviparous, which mean they produce live young. Rattlesnake habitats range all the way from Saskatchewan, Canada, to Argentina in South America.

Rattlesnake venom is cloudy and mostly made of proteins. Venoms have neurotoxic elements that affect the nervous system of victims.

Photo, facing page, Animals Animals © Joe McDonald

SNAKES

RHINOCEROUS VIPER (*Bitis nasicornis*)

In the forests of Central Africa, the colorful rhinocerous viper coils, ready to strike with its extremely large fangs. Once venom is injected into prey, the snake tracks down its dying victim and then swallows it whole. Can you imagine swallowing a chicken or a cow (or even a stalk of broccoli) whole? Of course, such a thing would be impossible for us humans, but some snakes can swallow a small deer whole. How can they get so much food into their mouth at one time? Snake jaws are specially designed for big mouthfuls. The bone that connects the lower jaw to the snake's skull works like a double-jointed hinge: the jaw drops open at the back and at the front. Also, the two bones of the lower jaw can stretch sideways because the chin muscles are very elastic.

Still hard to believe? Sharp teeth curving toward the snake's throat keep prey in place. Shifting its jaws side to side, bite by bite, the snake then "walks" its mouth over its victim.

Rhinocerous vipers—some of the most colorful true vipers—have skin that is purple and blue with green triangles. This irregular geometric pattern blends in amazingly with leaves on the forest floor. These vipers are named for large scales covering the tip of their snout, which can be raised to an erect position.

If you are bitten by a venomous snake, you should receive medical attention as soon as possible. Long ago, people believed that holding "snake stones" (made of animal bone or horn) against a wound would cure snakebites. Unfortunately, they were wrong.

True vipers are found in Europe, Asia, and Africa.

Photo, facing page, Animals Animals © Joe McDonald

S N A K E S

ASIATIC COBRAS (*Naja naja* group)

Cobras, coral snakes, mambas and sea snakes are members of a group of extremely dangerous venomous snakes that have venom-conducting fangs fixed at the front end of their jaw. The other group of extremely dangerous venomous snakes have much larger folding fangs that tuck backward when they are not in use.

Southeast Asia, Africa, and India are cobra country. Asiatic cobras are not aggressive. You might say they don't go looking for trouble, but if trouble comes their way, watch out! Cobra venom is so potent it can cause death in humans and other large animals; about 10 percent of cobra bites are fatal. Most cobra attacks on humans happen at night, in the dark, when people accidentally step on snakes.

To avoid trouble, cobras use a defensive, or warning, posture that warns other animals to stay away. The Asiatic cobra has very long ribs that can push out its neck skin like a hood. When the hood is fully displayed, it is much wider than the snake's body. In defensive posture, one-third of the cobra's body rises straight up while the rest is coiled.

Cobras are famous as the snake charmer's snake of choice. How do snake charmers train their snakes? They don't. Snakes can't learn tricks, but they can be handled by humans. Snake charmers cool their snakes down before a show. A cool snake is slow and passive—and easier to handle. Unfortunately, many human "charmers" do not treat their snakes in a humane way.

King cobras are famous for a very weird moan. They are also the world's largest cobra, but they usually attack humans only when they are provoked or when their nest is threatened. The female king cobra is the only cobra that builds her own nest. She makes a crook in the forepart of her body and drags leaves and sticks into a pile. Her eggs go on the bottom compartment, and then the female (and sometimes the male) stands guard on the upper compartment.

S N A K E S

PÉRINGUEY'S ADDER (*Bitus peringueyi*)

Péringuey's adders and their relatives are some of the deadliest snakes in Africa. Although their venom does not work as quickly as that of a cobra or a mamba, it is powerful enough to kill.

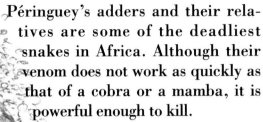

Péringuey's adders are also known as puff adders. They are so named for their ability to huff and puff—a warning to potential predators. Puff adders are called "sidewinders" because they have a unique way of traveling over sand; this form of sidewinding locomotion leaves a telltale trail. Adders lift loop after loop of their body free and clear of the surface. This form of locomotion is best for cruising across soft sand and dunes.

A puff adder has a very large head to make room for extremely large venom glands. Its body and tail are short—puff adders grow to a length of about 1 to 1.25 meters (3 to 4 feet)—and the péringuey's adder is even shorter.

Some adders would rather flee than fight, and they may vanish before your very eyes. Does that sound like magic? Some species are nifty burrowers, and they can disappear below desert sand in less than a minute.

The Péringuey's adder is a true viper, a member of the scientific family *Viperidae*. The world's smallest vipers may be less than 30 centimeters (1 foot) long, while the largest—the gaboon—may reach a length of 1.8 meters (6 feet) and a width of 15.24 centimeters (6 inches)!

The four most common methods of snake locomotion are serpentine motion, rectilinear motion, concertina motion, and sidewinding. During serpentine motion, the snake pushes its body against uneven ground. Rectilinear motion is slooowww motion; belly scales provide traction. When the snake bunches and straightens its muscles to move forward, it is using the concertina method of locomotion. You already know about sidewinding.

Photo, facing page, Animals Animals © Anthony Bannister

S N A K E S

BRAZILIAN RAINBOW BOA (*Epicrates cenchris*)

Boas are known for their extremely colorful and iridescent skin. This rainbow coloring might seem like the last thing snakes could hide behind, but that's exactly what they do. Orange, yellow, and black patterned Brazilian rainbow boas become almost invisible when sunlight dapples the leaves in their forest habitats in South and Central America. In the right light, you can't see the snakes for the trees.

It is just as difficult to pick out one Brazilian rainbow boa from all the others when they cluster together. Adult boas sometimes form clusters during the mating season. These boas are viviparous, which means they bear live young rather than lay eggs.

Pythons and boas are deaf, but they can "feel" loud noises with their tongues. In fact, a snake's tongue is three sense organs in one: it can touch, smell, and hear.

In cooler northern climates, some garter snakes crowd or coil together in dens to stay warm during winter hibernation. Although the snakes do cool over time, heat loss is reduced.

Photo, facing page, Animals Animals © Paul Freed

S N A K E S

MEXICAN CANTIL (*Agkistrodon bilineatus*)

Mexican cantils are pit vipers—just like rattlesnakes and fer-de-lances—and they use their special pit organ to locate and accurately strike and inject venom into their prey. But Mexican cantils are different from many of their relatives because they sometimes do much of their hunting near or in water.

The Mexican cantil feeds on fish, frogs, birds, and small animals along lakeshores and stream banks in Mexico and farther south. It is also known as the Mexican moccasin, and it is a relative of the North American water moccasin.

In skin pattern, a young cantil resembles yet another type of pit viper, the copperhead, with its bright yellow bands and yellow-tipped tail. The tail comes in very handy; when it is slowly wiggled, it acts as a lure for curious prey.

Mexican cantils retain their bold coloring when they are adults, but they develop different patterns. They also sport a blood-red forked tongue. They may reach a length of 1.5 meters (5 feet), and their body is thick.

Another pit viper, the eyelash viper, is named for the horny scales—a scaly eyelash—above its eyes. Because they are often found in tropical fruit trees, especially banana trees, eyelash pit vipers have accidentally traveled to many parts of the world on banana boats.

Photo, facing page, Animals Animals © Joe McDonald

S N A K E S

AFRICAN EGG-EATING SNAKE (*Dasypeltis scabra*)

You've probably eaten an egg for breakfast, but have you swallowed the shell, too? African egg-eating snakes are egg specialists. They eat only birds' eggs that are hard-shelled. Their mouth and neck are amazingly expandable and flexible. In fact, they may swallow an egg that is twice as wide as their body! The bones in their neck and back are long and sharp and spiny and act as a saw. As the snake swallows, the egg passes though the throat and is pushed up against the neck bones; the shell is cracked and crushed.

Using muscle power, the snake squeezes the contents of the egg all the way to its stomach. The snake curves its body to force the shell and membrane back to the mouth, where they are spit out or regurgitated.

Egg-eating snakes can devour as many eggs as they find at one time. It may take only minutes or as long as an hour to eat an egg.

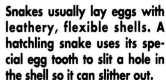

Many snakes can eat the soft-shelled eggs laid by lizards and some snakes, but devouring hard-shelled eggs is the job of only a few snakes.

Snakes usually lay eggs with leathery, flexible shells. A hatchling snake uses its special egg tooth to slit a hole in the shell so it can slither out.

Photo, facing page, Animals Animals © Michael Fogden

S N A K E S

SOUTHERN BANDED WATER SNAKE (*Nerodia fasciata pictiventris*)

Swamps, marshes, and dark slow streams of Florida, South Carolina, and Alabama are favorite places for southern banded water snakes to cruise. They are active during the day, but they are often seen basking on branches overhanging water. When disturbed, they drop instantly into the water for a quick getaway.

The southern banded water snake feeds mostly on small fish such as minnows. This is a large, heavy-bodied snake, and adults may reach a length of 1.8 meters (6 feet). Although the newly born young are only about 20 centimeters (8 inches) long, they make up for their size in number; there may be 100 or more young per birth!

What's in a common name? Cotton-mouthed snakes are named for the cottony color of their open mouth. Southern banded water snakes are named for their markings. Milk snakes are so named because some folks used to believe they actually "milked" cows.

Southern banded water snakes can be found in Florida's Everglades. Among the other animals found in this amazing area are alligators, rare birds, and plants that grow nowhere else.

Photo, facing page, Animals Animals © Joe McDonald

S N A K E S

SEA SNAKE (Family: *Hydrophidae*)

Sea snakes—relatives of cobras and coral snakes—are among the most venemous of all snakes. They live mostly in tropical coastal waters of Asia and Australia; they are never found in the Atlantic Ocean. Some species of sea snakes produce live young at sea, while other species come ashore long enough to lay their eggs. All are adapted for life in the ocean.

A sea snake can stay underwater for as long as five hours at a time. In order to swim quickly, it has a flattened, oar-like tail. It is also equipped with valvelike nostrils that control the flow of seawater. (After all, it doesn't have fingers to plug its nose.) The sea snake has a slender head—the better to squeeze into tight spaces to search for eels, its main prey.

There are about fifty different species of sea snakes. The species pictured here lives in Australia's Coral Sea.

Some sea snakes reach a length of 2.4 meters (8 feet) or more!

SHAMROCK SPIDER (Family: Araneidae)

The shamrock—named for a clover-shaped spot on its abdomen—might be a lucky spider. Part of a large group called orb weavers, shamrock spiders are often busy spinning nifty circular webs between bushes and vines and tall grasses throughout North America.

Female shamrocks reach sizes of a half-inch. Males are much smaller—one-fifth of an inch. Both are famous for spinning amazing geometric webs in a step-by-step process. First, a basic scaffold of mooring lines is set down by the spider. Then, the radial lines, like bicycle spokes, are added. Finally, the spider begins the circular pattern, working from the inside out to the largest circumference.

Young orb weavers don't go to school to learn weaving; instead, they follow their instincts. With no training from adult spiders, even the tiniest, freshly hatched spiderling knows how to spin silk and weave webs.

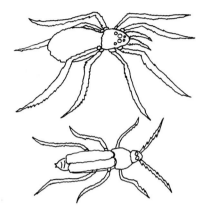

Spiders are not insects. There are many differences between the two, but the most obvious is that spiders have eight walking legs while insects only have six. Insects also have one pair of antenna and often have wings, but spiders have none.

Spiders, scorpions, mites, sea spiders, insects, crustaceans, and horseshoe crabs all belong to the same scientific phylum, Arthropoda. Together, they make up more than 900,000 species. Arachnids are arthropods who have four pairs of legs and no wings. They number about 70,000 species. A single group of arachnids, spiders, boast a mere 35,000 species.

SPIDERS

286

GIANT WOLF SPIDER (Family: Lycosidae)

Giant wolf spiders are wonderfully hairy, and their eyes are very big, all eight of them! Four smallish eyes are set low on the spider's face, a large pair of eyes sits above them and points straight ahead, while farther back, two big eyes look up like tiny searchlights. This eye design means the wolf spider can see in four directions at once and spy moving creatures at a distance of 3 to 4 inches. That's a pretty long way for spiders.

All wolf spiders are excellent hunters. They are fast and strong, pouncing on victims and then crushing and biting them. The bodies of giant wolf spiders grow to lengths of one and one-half inches, and these ground-dwelling creatures can be found almost anywhere in the world—they're not fussy about where they set up house.

Female wolf spiders are devoted mothers who wrap their eggs in a silken sac that they drag along with them everywhere. After about three weeks, spiderlings emerge when the female bites open the sac. These tiny spiders climb onto their mother's back, and there they stay for a week while she hunts and even battles other creatures. Spider babies must cling tight for the ride or they will be left behind. After the spiderlings molt (shed their outer skin), they are ready to begin a hunter's life on their own.

Spiders don't eat dinner, they drink it. After catching prey, spiders inject venom to paralyze the victim. They then regurgitate digestive juices over the prey so that it becomes liquid and drinkable. Sometimes, spiders start "drinking" before their victim is dead.

Why are all those weird people dancing the tarantella? In the 1500s and 1600s, big European wolf spiders were wrongly blamed for causing the nervous disease, "tarantism." Once bitten, people supposedly began dancing wildly, the only cure. Actually, the bite of a European wolf spider is harmless. History buffs still wonder what caused all the fuss? It could have been another spider, but, more likely, some people's imaginations got carried away. Or, maybe they just felt like dancing.

SPIDERS

BLACK WIDOW (Family: Theridiidae)

Around the world, there is a group of shiny black spiders recognized by their bright red markings and feared for their venom that attacks the nervous system. In some areas, they are commonly called black wolf spiders, hourglass spiders, and shoe-button spiders. In North America, this spider goes by the name of black widow, and the female is one of the most poisonous of all spiders.

Although the black widow has a scary reputation, she's actually very shy and passive, hunting only for food. She likes to build her web in, on, or close to the ground where it will snag passing insects. When the black widow feels someone tugging on the web, she comes out of hiding and approaches with care. Using her hind legs, she draws fresh silk from her spinnerets and binds up the struggling victim. Now, the spider is ready to inject her venom by piercing the victim's leg with her minute, needle-sharp fangs. While the insect still struggles, the black widow begins to hoist it into the air with her silken system of pulleys, until it finally reaches a height of three inches. Then, the victim can be moved to a convenient place deep in the spider's maze. Feasting for three or four days, the spider eventually sucks her prey dry until only a shell remains to be tossed away somewhere inside the mazelike web.

Although the black widow only bites humans when she feels her life is threatened, her bite is very dangerous. Learn to be on the lookout for this spider in wood piles and under rocks.

Spider silk is truly amazing. Some spider webs, stretched into a single line, would reach for more than 300 miles. Although webs are an important part of a spider's life, these tiny critters also use silk to drift on air currents at altitudes of 2,500 feet, to protect their eggs, and even to flirt! Male spiders pluck out a rhythm on the strings of a female's web to win her favor.

Photo, facing page, courtesy Animals Animals © Raymond A. Mendez

SPIDERS

HAIRY TARANTULA (Family: Theraphosidae)

When they need to grow, all spiders do it the hard way—shedding their outer too-tight skeleton (or cuticle) in exchange for a whole new suit of clothes—in a process called "molting." Although molting is risky and dangerous for spiders, they have no say in the matter. It's part of their natural behavior. But it is the time they are most vulnerable to their enemies.

The biggest American tarantulas usually begin this risky business in late summer. They refuse to eat and become very sloowww. Their bodies look dull and worn out because they're sporting last year's hairy skin.

Tarantulas spend several hours spinning a special molting bed, a soft sheet of silk, to lie on. With front and hind legs attached to the bed and lying on their backs, the spider looks almost dead. It takes two or three hours before the old cuticle begins to split along the sides and back of the spider's body. Then, rhythmical cramps help the spider pull its new legs from their old case—front legs first. In a shiny new cuticle (complete with a full set of hairs), the tarantula now lies quietly for two to three hours to toughen up. While this fresh cuticle is still soft, the spider can grow noticeably in size.

Within the spider community, the number of molts depends on the size of the spider. The smallest spiders only molt five or six times. Male tarantulas sometimes molt more than 20 times in their life, and females claim the record at 30 or 40 times! Most spiders stop molting once they reach sexual maturity, but tarantulas are long lived and primitive as spiders go, so they molt even after they're fully grown.

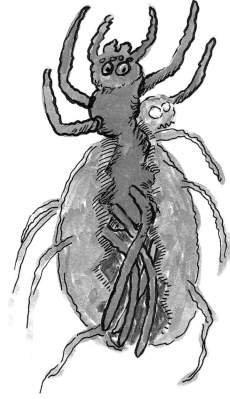

Arthropods don't have skeletons inside their bodies. Instead, they're encased in a hard outer shell. Because this outer skeleton doesn't grow, spiders and other arthropods must shed their skeleton suit from time to time, in order to increase their size. This process is called "molting."

Molting spiders are hard to find because they try to molt in private, very protected places.

Photo, facing page, courtesy Animals Animals © Marshall Black/OSF

SPIDERS

GOLDENROD SPIDER (Family: Thomisidae)

The goldenrod spider might not be showing its true colors, because it's actually white! The truth is, this pretty spider changes color from white to yellow depending on the flowers in the background. Goldenrod spiders (and other varieties of flower spiders) spend most of their lives in the heads of flowers. There, they lie in wait ready to ambush flying insects that are in search of flower nectar.

Big, fierce bugs—bees, wasps, large-winged butterflies—are captured by these pygmy ambushers.

Scientists have discovered that flying insects avoid light-colored blossoms that have dark spots resembling spiders. If they want to catch dinner, flower spiders must color-coordinate with their background. Goldenrod spiders are masters of camouflage; in one week's time, they can turn from white to yellow. In 4 or 5 days, they can return to white. This ability allows them to hunt from either yellow or white blossoms.

Spiders secrete a sticky mucous that they "glue" onto certain areas of their web. After a day or two, this glue is no longer sticky, so the spider eats its web and spins a brand-new one from scratch.

Photo, facing page, courtesy Animals Animals © Breck P. Kent

SPIDERS

JUMPING SPIDER (Family: Salticidae)

This massive and hairy critter is a jumpy member of the largest group of American jumping spiders. With brightly colored bodies, curly beards, and bands of shimmering scales, jumping spiders are rainbow bright. They can be especially proud of their stylish legs, fringed with plumes of red, orange, or yellow hairs.

Male jumping spiders use their front legs to charm females during the mating season. Almost dancing, they sway and sashay in a zigzag pattern designed to show off the glory of their plumes and the iridescent gleam of their scales. Male charm is especially important because female jumping spiders are known for their bad tempers. Approaching and retreating with their dance steps, male spiders must time their courting techniques perfectly, or they could end up as the female's dinner instead of her mate.

Most spiders mate once a year when the weather is warmest, but they can produce more than one egg sac per mating. Indeed, true spiders have a life span of only one or two years, so they may only mate twice in a lifetime.

Spiders have a nifty way of moving to new locations—via silken parachutes. From a high blade of grass, flower, or fence post, the spider stands on the tips of its legs, abdomen toward the sky. From the spinnerets, many silken strands travel up on air currents until they are buoyant enough to lift the spider up, up, and away (sometimes as high as 5,000 feet). Spiders are known to travel hundreds of miles by "ballooning." In this way, they pioneer new habitats. Of course, ballooning has a down side: spiders never know where they will land!

Jumping spiders are eight-legged athletes able to leap ten inches at a time. If you were an extremely big (and weird) jumping spider, you could jump 40 feet!

SPIDERS

Photo, facing page, courtesy Animals Animals © E.R. Degginger

FISHING SPIDER (Family: Pisauridae)

Big-eyed fishing spiders are pond-skaters, able to skim over the water's surface because their bodies are extremely light compared to their size. Tiny hairs, sticky and plentiful on their legs, also help provide buoyancy and traction when skating. Because they are balloon light, fishing spiders can't dive or stay underwater unless they attach themselves to leaves. Like many spiders, fishing spiders can use an air bubble for underwater breathing—but only for a very short time.

True to their name, sharp-eyed fishing spiders are known to catch very small minnows and tadpoles for dinner. Their system is to perch their two back legs on a small stone, rock, or twig and cast their other six legs out over the water. When a tadpole cruises by, the fishing spider plunges suddenly underwater and wraps its legs around the startled prey. After a great struggle, the tadpole is lugged back onto the perch and devoured.

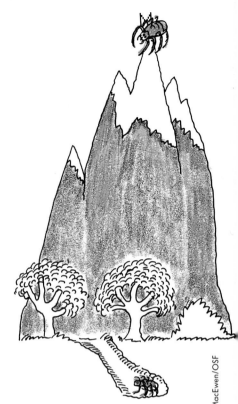

Spiders live in almost every nook and cranny of the world, below ground and above. Indeed, spiders have been found above altitudes of 20,000 feet on Mount Everest.

SPIDERS

CRAB SPIDER (Family: Thomisidae)

All spiders can lose a leg or two without feeling the pinch. This ability is called "autotomy," and it comes in handy to escape tricky situations—especially when somebody else wants to eat you for dinner. Mature spiders must do without lost limbs, but young spiders (those still molting) can regrow legs that work almost like new.

Nimble crab spiders can manage minus one, two, or even three legs and still escape the clutches of an enemy on the run. Since front legs in crab spiders are important organs of touch as well as weapons of attack, catching flies is a real problem without them. When both front legs are left behind, crab spiders simply aim the next pair in a forward direction.

In order to autotomize a leg, spiders need something to push against. When a predator grabs a spider by one leg, that leg will snap loose at its weakest point if the spider is able to hold onto a twig or a leaf. If the spider is held in the air, it must push itself away from the predator or it won't be able to lose its leg and escape to safety.

If a spider is bitten by a predator that only breaks the cuticle of a leg, the spider will probably bleed to death. To save its life, a spider instinctually amputates the wounded leg. To do this, it uses its mouth and other legs to pull the leg off, or it spins threads attached to its leg and pulls against them. After amputation, spiders suck the leg dry.

Sticky, tacky hairs on spiders' feet keep them from slipping and sliding when they land after a jump. These hairs are also handy for scaling slick surfaces.

Photo, facing page, courtesy Animals Animals © Richard Shiell

SPIDERS

BLACK AND YELLOW GARDEN SPIDER (Family: Araneidae)

The plump black and yellow garden spider spins her two-foot-wide web over shrubs, flowers, and other handy garden plants. Even in a heat wave, she can be found perched proudly in the center of her webby kingdom like a black and yellow bull's-eye. Grasshoppers are a favorite meal, although a variety of flying insects whizz in for dinner. Like many garden spiders, the black and yellow is a skilled spinner, and she uses her silk for several jobs. Besides building her home and hunting, this spider deposits her eggs inside a soft silken sac and hangs it from a nearby shrub. Silk is a spider's all-purpose tool.

Spider silk is extremely amazing stuff. A super protein produced as a liquid in special silk glands located in the spider's abdomen, silk hardens as it is stretched from the spinnerets. Spider silk might look delicate, but the relative tension needed to break it is far greater than for steel. And there's more than one type of silk. The spider uses non-stick silk for radial web lines and sticky silk for the spiraling circles. Also, some silk is ultraviolet to attract insects.

Spiders are as old as the hills. In fact, they are some of the earliest of earth's land predators, dating back at least 380 million years. Scientists can keep their dates straight because a fossil spinneret—no bigger than a pin head—was recently discovered in New York state. Of course, we all know that spinnerets are teensy raised openings found on a spider's rear end. Through these openings, liquid spider silk becomes the stuff webs are made of.

Photo, facing page, courtesy Animals Animals © Charlie Palek

SPIDERS

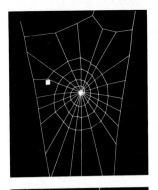

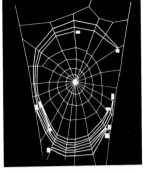

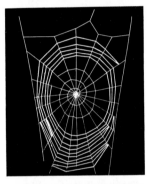

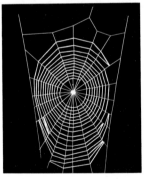

Models showing the process of weaving the web of *Eperia sericata (sclopettaria)* (Neg. No. 37859; Photo R.C. Lenskjold; Courtesy Department Library Services, American Museum of Natural History)

OGRE-FACED STICK SPIDER (Family: Dinopidae)

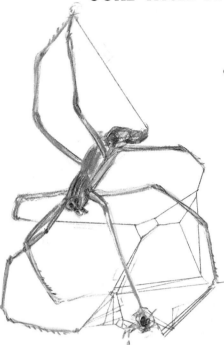

With two out of eight eyes like giant head-lamps, stiltlike legs, a humped body that could pass for a thorn, a twig, or a bud, and an odd head, the ogre-faced stick spider looks extremely weird. But looks aren't everything, and this spider is famed for casting its silky "net" over flying prey. For this reason, some people call it the net-casting spider.

Ogre-faced stick spiders spend their days pressed flat against the bark of a tree limb with their front legs stretched out and their back legs holding firm around the branch. This strange perch makes it very hard for passing predators to spot them. But after sundown, it's another story.

The ogre-faced spider begins each evening's work by first spinning a small rectangular net about the size of a postage stamp. The spider holds the little net with its four front legs and uses its back legs to hang onto the main web. Hanging downward, ogre-face waits for the right moment to cast itself forward, with its net stretched 5 or 6 times normal size to catch a passing insect. The unfortunate prey is instantly paralyzed with spider venom, then wrapped in silk and eaten. This same method and net are used all night. When the ogre-faced spider is full, or daylight arrives, it neatly rolls its net into a ball and drops it to the ground.

Step into my parlor, said the spider to the fly. Why do bugs fly into spider webs? Maybe they really are invited. Scientists have recently discovered that some spiders decorate their webs with silk strands that reflect ultraviolet light. And, what do you know, webs with ultraviolet strands attract more bugs than webs without. Apparently, for bugs, ultraviolet light is a sign of the clear blue sky.

SPIDERS

Photo, facing page, courtesy Animals Animals © OSF

SPINED SPIDER (Family: Araneidae)

Clinging from the center of its web, the tropical spined spider might easily be mistaken for a wood chip, a flower, or some strange, exotic fruit. This short-legged spider relies on camouflage as well as its tough, leathery abdomen and colorful spines to discourage lizards, birds, and other predators from taking a spiky mouthful. But even sharp spines don't protect these spiders from wasps. Spider wasps sting their victims and carry the bodies back to line their nests. That way, wasp larva have plenty of spider bodies to eat.

Spined spiders use a special decoy to catch fly-eating insects. They decorate their web with little tufts of silk that look like tiny midge flies. When insects stop by for a "fly bite," they are trapped in the web instead.

Male spined spiders are pygmies compared to females. Small size comes in handy for males when they're courting and mating with short-tempered females—they're almost too small to be noticed, or eaten!

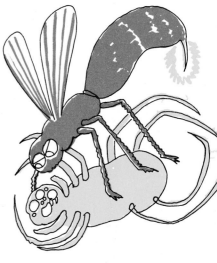

Wasps are dangerous to many spiders! Spider wasps are deadly to tarantulas; the big spiders hardly ever survive an encounter with this foe. This wasp crawls into a tarantula's burrow and stings the spider after a fierce battle—both rolling over and over. When stung, the spider is paralyzed. Alive but helpless, the giant spider is dragged to a grave dug by the wasp. The wasp deposits her egg inside the spider's abdomen and fills the grave with dirt. The spider may stay alive for months providing fresh food for the wasp larvae after they hatch.

Photo, facing page, courtesy Animals Animals © George K. Bryce

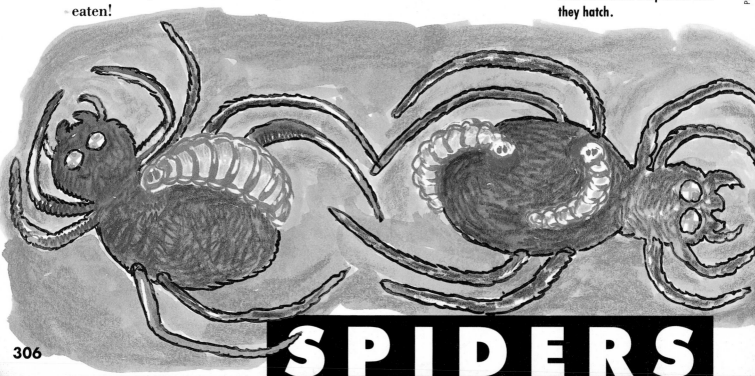

SPIDERS

WANDERING SPIDER (Family: Ctenidae)

Wandering spiders do exactly that— they wander far from home to do their hunting. They are not attached to webs (like web weavers), and they don't rely on silk. In the past, some of these spiders—like the big orange wandering spider from the tropics of South America— have hitched rides to North America on banana boats, but these days new shipping methods discourage uninvited spider guests. In fact, many spider species have been transported from one place to another by humans. If they like the climate when they arrive, they often stay and raise families.

Another wandering spider, Phoneutria, from South American jungles, has a bite that's as bad as its bark. Hairy giants, these aggressive spiders look scary, and their powerful venom, acting on the nervous system, can be fatal.

The largest wandering spiders have a diet that includes frogs, lizards, mice, and even snakes. Of course, they don't say no to insects.

Many American Indian tribes view the wily spider with great respect. For the Dakotah, a perfect orb web symbolizes the heavens. In Pueblo myths of the Southwest, a spider created the first woman and the first man. In Cherokee folklore, a brave and tiny spider brought the gift of fire to the rest of the animals. Spider Woman gave the art of blanket- and basket-weaving to the Navajo.

Spiderman uses the skills of a spider to climb walls, jump from building to building, and trap the bad guys! This comic book superhero is now part of popular American folklore.

SPIDERS

NURSERY WEB SPIDER (Family: Pisauridae)

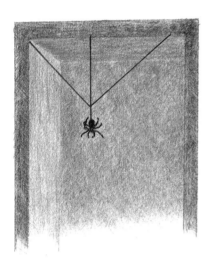

Molting is a dangerous business for true spiders just like it is for tarantulas. This is the time they are most helpless and vulnerable to predators. This is also the time when spiders grow.

All eight legs begin lengthening as they're pulled from their old skeleton, or cuticle. Youngsters molt and lengthen their legs in less than 30 minutes, but older spiders may take as long as two hours. It isn't uncommon for spiders to get stuck inside their old cuticle. In that case, they will die. But if all goes well, the spider begins a series of "calisthenics" once the new legs are free. These exercises keep the spider's joints from stiffening.

After the nursery web spider completes its final molt (it could molt as many as 13 times!), it will be a mature adult ready to mate. The nursery web female is a wonderful mother. Her first job is to spin a silken cover over her eggs. Once complete, the mother totes her egg sac *everywhere* until the spiderlings emerge. The sac is attached to her chelicerae in front and moored with silk to her behind. After the spiderlings hatch, the female ties the sac to a bunch of leaves. Now she begins to remodel, pulling the leaves over with silk until she makes a very nifty "parachute." The mother hangs over the outside of this parachute nursery until her spiderlings are old enough to leave the nest.

Scientists have been studying spider's silk because it is such amazing stuff. They have even isolated the gene responsible for silk production. Some silk is sticky, some isn't. It's amazingly strong and flexible. Spider silk has even been used as cross-hairs in rifles.

Moths and butterflies rarely get stuck in a spider's web. That's because the scales on their wings are nonstick when it comes to spider silk.

SPIDERS

SUN SPIDER (Family: Solpugidae)

When is a spider not a spider? When it's a spider—a close relative, but not a real spider. This arachnid has eight legs, just like spiders, as well as pedipalps and chelicerae. But it only sports two eyes, while most spiders have eight, or at least six.

In some ways, the sun spider might seem more like another arachnid, the scorpion. In fact, it is sometimes called a wind scorpion. But its pedipalps are not pincers, and it boasts no stinger.

It's not easy to figure out just who belongs where. For instance, the daddy longlegs spider isn't a spider. If you look at its body closely you may see lots of wrinkles but only one body part. There is no waist or obvious joint on a daddy longleg's body. Also, while spiders are usually solitary creatures, daddy longlegs often hang out in groups.

Unlike most spiders, Stegodyphus community spiders from southern Africa are groupies. They build, repair, and share an amazing web that can cover four yards square! Within their silken kingdom, community spiders use teamwork to handle flying ants, beetles, and grasshoppers (some are tens of times bigger than the spiders!) caught in the web. All Stegodyphus seem to share the work load, and the community spirit allows these spiders to maximize their hunting and spinning skills and to survive in a harsh environment. But a Stegodyphus web is not for commmity spiders alone. This micro-universe also houses lazy parasite spiders, wasp and moth larvae, and even a small mouse or two.

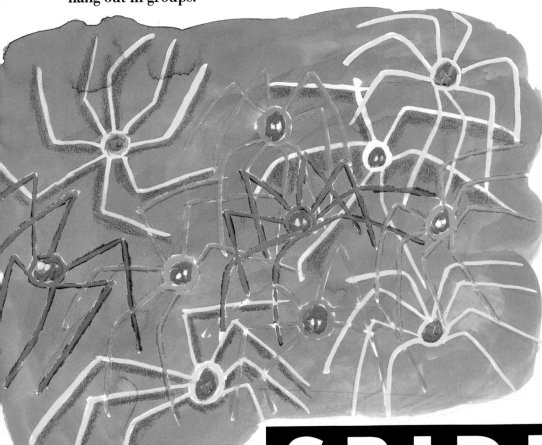

SPIDERS

BIRD-DROPPING SPIDER (Family: Thomisidae)

Three guesses what the bird-dropping spider looks like! This little crab spider is one of a group that protect themselves by looking like something no one wants to eat. Some are perfect imitations of tiny seeds, leaves, or flowers. But the Malaysian bird-dropping spider has one of the most unusual costumes of all, and it is especially convincing when perched on its web.

For spiders, camouflage works two ways—to discourage predators and to attract prey. When spiders are in disguise, predators like lizards, wasps, and birds may pass them by. But critters that spiders love to eat may think they see a bird dropping when it's really a hungry spider.

Another spider that sometimes imitates a bird dropping is the female bolas spider. This incredible huntress hangs by her back legs from a few strands of silk. With her front legs, she holds a silk line with a sticky blob at the end and waits for a moth to fly by. When her prey is within range, the bolas spider throws her silk line at the moth, "sticks it," and hauls it in to eat.

Australian Aborigines have long used a unique method of fly fishing. Poking the end of a pole into a sticky spider's web, the angler creates a long line of silk. This is dipped into the crushed body of a large silk spider. The rest of the spider's body and the fishing line are tossed into a stream where fish gather. As the fish bite at the scraps, their mouths are tangled in the silk and they are pulled to shore.

Photo, facing page, courtesy Animals Animals © OSF

SPIDERS

This glossarized index will help you find specific information on animals. It will also help you understand the meaning of some of the words used in this book.